ELEMENTAL DISCOURSES

THE COLLECTED WRITINGS OF JOHN SALLIS

Elemental Discourses

THE COLLECTED WRITINGS OF JOHN SALLIS

VOLUME II/4

JOHN SALLIS

INDIANA UNIVERSITY PRESS

This book is a publication of

Indiana University Press
Office of Scholarly Publishing
Herman B Wells Library 350
1320 East 10th Street
Bloomington, Indiana 47405 USA

iupress.indiana.edu

© 2018 by John Sallis
All rights reserved

No part of this book may be reproduced or utilized in any form or by any means, electronic or mechanical, including photocopying and recording, or by any information storage and retrieval system, without permission in writing from the publisher. The paper used in this publication meets the minimum requirements of the American National Standard for Information Sciences—Permanence of Paper for Printed Library Materials, ANSI Z39.48–1992.

Manufactured in the United States of America

Cataloging information is available from the Library of Congress.

ISBN 978-0-253-03722-0 (hardback)
ISBN 978-0-253-03723-7 (pbk.)
ISBN 978-0-253-03724-4 (web PDF)

1 2 3 4 5   23 22 21 20 19 18

CONTENTS

1. VOICES — 1

2. GATHERING LANGUAGE — 20

3. THE PLAY OF TRANSLATION — 37

4. THINGS OF SENSE — 52

5. ARCHAIC NATURE — 66

6. ALTERITY AND THE ELEMENTAL — 84

7. OBJECTIVITY AND THE REACH OF ENCHORIAL SPACE — 99

8. THE SCOPE OF VISIBILITY — 122

9. COSMIC TIME — 138

10. THE NEGATIVITY OF TIME-SPACE — 153

AFTERWORD — 173

Index of Prinicpal Names   175

ELEMENTAL DISCOURSES

1 VOICES

There are perhaps no powers that appear more manifestly and directly reflexive than the voice. The possibility of duplicity—of doubling and even of concealing the doubling—is by no means excluded: one can mimetically assume the voice of another or even lend one's voice to another as in ventriloquy. However, when one speaks in one's own voice, perhaps also attesting even that it is in one's own voice that one is speaking, then the seemingly direct reflexivity of the voice becomes operative. Then speech displays, precisely in this reflexivity, the character of ownness, and it is no longer openly marked by duplicity in either sense.

The reflexivity is perhaps most readily manifest in the word itself.

To say the word is to invoke immediately that which the word names. In the very voicing of the word *voice*, one instantiates what it means or at least attests to the power that it names. In being voiced, in sounding forth from the voice, the word performs what it names. In being uttered, it reflects back upon the utterance in such a way as to affirm their coincidence across the difference between word and deed, λόγος and ἔργον.

Yet, reflexivity is also manifest in the very operation of the voice, quite aside from its engagement with the word. In this regard it can be compared to phantasy or even, more obliquely, to imagination. In the respective operations of the voice and of phantasy, production and reception are bound together in the most intimate connection. With regard to this structure, both the voice and phantasy can, in turn, be compared to original or intellectual intuition as this concept was posited by Kant. Intuition of this kind is—or would be, if it were—such that "the existence [*Dasein*] of the object of intuition is given through it itself"[1]—that is, through the intuition itself. In contrast to the derivative intuition belonging to all finite creatures, original intuition could be ascribed only to the primordial being (*Urwesen*). For such a being, the very intuition of something would coincide with its production—that is, as with phantasy and the voice, production—of images, of sounds, of objects—and intuitive reception of what is produced are bound together, either in intimate connection or, in the case of the primordial being, in absolute identity. Just as for the primordial being, intuition is bound to production, so in giving voice to an utterance I hear directly the utterance voiced; in speaking I hear myself speaking—indeed with such immediacy that the difference between the production and the reception of vocal sound appears to be completely dissolved.

The structural affinity between the voice thus regarded in its reflexivity and original intuition as the absolute identity of intuition and production point to the situatedness of this construal of the voice within the history of metaphysics. In effect, the construal of the voice as directly reflexive, as given back in its very sounding forth, envisions it as imaging the absolute reflexivity of the primordial being, for whom being an object is absolutely identical with being present to intuition. In other words, the voice is conceived within the compass of the identity of being and being present—that is, within the orbit of being as presence. In regarding this as the orbit in which metaphysics turns in the course of its history, it is imperative to observe that the word *metaphysics* floats undecidably between singular and plural. While the single determination of being as presence can—though not without discontinuities—be traced in the history of metaphysics, there are also multiple instances where a turn is initiated against precisely this determination, often even within the very affirmation of it. If this history can be regarded as the history of being—and this itself remains open to question—it is also, perhaps preeminently, the history of a thinking that can turn freely against the alleged destiny of being and interrupt its uniformity.

The philosophical concept of the voice belongs to this history, even though it assumes various guises. Yet, already in the Greek understanding of φωνή a certain breach of unity, a dispersion into different senses, can be observed. The most fully articulated sense is found

---

1. I. Kant, *Kritik der reinen Vernunft*, vol. 3 of *Werke: Akademie Textausgabe* (Berlin: Walter de Gruyter, 1968), B72.

in Aristotle. In Book 2 of *De Anima*[2] he offers a series of four interconnected determinations; they are set amid various discussions of how certain sounds such as coughing and sounds made by certain animals such as fish must be distinguished from voice. The first determination is of such generality that it does not quite exclude all these cases. It reads: "Voice is sound produced by an ensouled being"—though, as he adds, not with just any bodily part. The second determination describes the production: "Voice consists in the impact of the inspired air on the so-called windpipe under the agency of the soul in those parts." The third determination states once again that the producer of the vocal sound must be ensouled, but it adds another, quite remarkable requirement: "It is necessary that that which causes the impact be ensouled and do so with some phantasy [μετὰ φαντασίας]." So, not only, as we have noted already, does phantasy exhibit a structural parallel with voice, but also, at least according to Aristotle's analysis, a certain exercise of phantasy belongs to voice, to the production of vocal sound. Without phantasy there would be only sound, no voice, not even if produced by an ensouled being. The final determination leaps entirely beyond all description of producer and production of voice, beyond to the operation of signification. It reads simply: "Voice is a sound that means something [σημαντικός—so: a signifying sound]." Aristotle does not draw a connection between the third and fourth determinations, specifically between the dependence of voice on phantasy and its capacity to mean something. However, one could readily suppose that phantasy serves to bring something into view—even though only, as we say, in the mind's eye—to bring it into view, to make it present, in such a way that in the sounding of the voice it can, in some register, be meant.

To the first of these determinations, which identifies voice as sound produced by an ensouled being, Aristotle adds another observation. He says that while inanimate things never make a vocal sound, there are certain things that can by virtue of similarity be said to do so; his examples are a flute and a lyre and indeed anything that has the characteristic features of a musical instrument. The similarity lies in the fact that voice also has these features, namely, musical range, tune, and modulation. Music is thus accorded a privileged relation to the voice. The affirmation of this relation, the reference of music as such to the voice, will remain decisive, even if covertly, until finally it is expressed explicitly in

---

2. Aristotle, *De Anima*, 420b6–34.

Hegel's *Aesthetics*—in these words: "The human voice contains the ideal totality of soundings, which is merely spread out among the other instruments in their particular differences."[3] In this legacy running from Aristotle to Hegel, there is thus operative in the philosophical conception of music what Derrida will call phonocentrism.

For Aristotle voice is a certain kind of sound; it is sound produced by a certain kind of being in a certain way so as to have a signifying capacity. And yet, the word φωνή is not univocal—is not spoken as only one voice—but has also other senses. Near the end of Plato's *Symposium*, at the point where Socrates has just finished the speech in which he lent his voice to Diotima, there is a disruption of the conversation. Along with a hammering at the door, the symposiasts also "heard the φωνή of the flute-girl"—not her voice of course but the sound of her flute. Then, it is reported, "they heard the φωνή of Alcibiades."[4] The sense is twofold: they heard the sound produced by Alcibiades, by his voice, his capacity to produce sound recognizable as his. The sense of voice as the power to produce a certain kind of sound—the sense that sounds most prominently in the English word *voice*—is still more explicit in a passage in Sophocles' *Electra*. In this passage Clytemnestra is upbraiding Electra for having spread the rumor that her deed—the murder of Agamemnon—was brutal and unjust. She defends her action by appealing to Agamemnon's sacrifice of Iphigenia, their daughter; and then having given her defense, she says that "if the dead girl had φωνή, she would agree."[5] In this instance, φωνή clearly names, not a certain kind of sound, but the capacity, the power to produce such sound. Furthermore, between these two senses of φωνή there is a reflexivity: to utter a vocal sound is to attest thereby to one's power to vocalize.

There is still a third sense of φωνή, evident, for instance, in Plato's *Critias*. In a passage in which Critias is about to relate an ancient story about the foes of Athens, he tells how Solon traveled to Egypt to recover the story. There he found that the Egyptians had written it down after translating it into their own φωνή. In turn, Solon, recovering the sense of the words, translated the story back into Greek, into his own φωνή, and then wrote it down. In this account, seemingly the original

---

3. G. W. F. Hegel, *Ästhetik* (West Berlin: Das europäische Buch, 1985), 2:291f.
4. Plato, *Symposium*, 212c–d.
5. Sophocles, *Electra*, 548.

philosophical account of translation,⁶ φωνή clearly means language in the sense of the Greek or the Egyptian language. Translating into a language is, in turn, linked to a subsequent writing. What gets translated into a certain language then gets written down in that language.

The word φωνή thus extends across a broad spectrum of what has to do with words, from the vocal sound to the writing in which it can be set down. The word thus encompasses various items that subsequently come to be regarded as opposites: speech and language, spoken word and written word, the inner power of speech and the vocalized word sounding forth into the space without. It would be difficult to say whether in the Greek understanding of φωνή the terms of these oppositions are thought together in an intrinsic unity or whether the oppositions that will emerge are already implicit as such in this understanding. In any case, the word φωνή serves to assemble virtually all the moments that will be taken up in what we call, in general terms, speech or language—or, more pointedly, voice. Already in the Greek word φωνή there are multiple voices. Already one can offer a certain interpretation—certainly not the only one—of the imperative that Derrida expresses in these words: "It is always necessary to be more than one in order to speak; several voices are necessary for that."⁷

It is in the text *Voice and Phenomenon* that Derrida addresses the question of the voice, specifically, of the conditions and limits of the reflexivity of the voice. Among the three texts published in 1967, Derrida accords a certain priority to *Voice and Phenomenon*. In an interview he later described it as the essay to which he was most attached. He grants even—referring to the three works of 1967—that "in a classical philosophical architecture *Voice and Phenomenon* would come first." On the other hand, he countered this classical gesture by referring to what he calls a "strange geometry" by which the other two texts from 1967, *Of Grammatology* and *Writing and Difference*, could be stapled in the middle of one another. Though *Voice and Phenomenon* is not directly implicated in this strange geometry, Derrida's remark that he "could

---

6. Plato, *Critias*, 113a. See my extended discussion in *On Translation* (Bloomington: Indiana University Press, 2002), 55–62.

7. Jacques Derrida, "Sauf le nom," in *On the Name* (Stanford: Stanford University Press, 1995), 35.

have bound it as a note to one or the other of the two works" entails that it too can be considered as engaged in this strange geometry.[8]

In *Voice and Phenomenon* the reflexivity of the voice is addressed from the outset. Initially and still in general terms, its operation is considered in relation to the problem, the Husserlian problem, of how to reconcile consciousness and language, that is, the self-presence of consciousness and the nonpresence, the difference, that language involves by virtue of substituting a sign for an intuited object and, even more decisively, by virtue of its foray as sound into the world. In other words, the problem is to find a means by which to admit the relation to language without introducing externality, nonpresence, difference into consciousness and thus violating its determination as self-presence. Husserl's solution to the problem is provided by his appeal to the voice. It is the voice, regarded phenomenologically, that has the capacity to preserve presence. It is because of the innermost character of the voice that one can speak without interrupting the self-presence of consciousness. While language involves much that is exterior, at its core, in the phenomenological voice, self-presence is preserved. Derrida writes: "Husserl will radicalize the necessary privilege of the *phonē*, which is implied by the whole history of metaphysics, and will exploit all its resources with the greatest critical refinement." What counts for Husserl, Derrida explains, lies "not in the sonorous or in the physical voice, in the body of the voice in the world . . . but in the phenomenological voice, in the voice in its transcendental flesh, in the breath, the intentional animation that transforms the body of the word into flesh." Derrida adds finally and most decisively: "The phenomenological voice would be this spiritual flesh that continues to speak and to be present to itself—to hear itself [*s'entendre*]—in the absence of the world."[9]

Thus, the phenomenological voice would be a speaking consciousness withdrawn from the nonpresence and exteriority that would otherwise be introduced by the involvement of speech in the world. It would be a consciousness that, in its very speaking, would be present to itself, would, without any exit outside, hear itself speaking. Husserl's procedure would consist, then, in internalizing speech to the point where, as the circuit of speaking-hearing-oneself-speaking, it becomes simply a

---

8. Derrida, *Positions* (Paris: Les Éditions de Minuit, 1972), 12f.
9. Derrida, *La Voix et le Phénomène* (Paris: Presses Universitaires de France, 1967), 15f.

moment of the self-presence of consciousness; all externality is reduced, and speech is assimilated to consciousness. In other words, speech is reduced to the pure reflexivity of the voice that, freed of all interference from without, hears itself speaking.

Now, it would seem, there are even more voices, at least one in addition to those heard already by the Greeks. For the phenomenological voice is neither the sonorous voice, that is, the sounding word, nor the physical voice, the vocalizing, sound-producing capacity, the power (as Aristotle describes it) to make the inspired air impact the windpipe. Both of these—the sounding word and the power of speech—require (as again Aristotle explains) the agency of the soul. Husserl would reduce the voice to this soulful agency, reconceived in modern philosophical terms. It is thus that he describes the phenomenological voice as intentional animation. Derrida's description is more provocative: he describes this voice as the transcendental or spiritual flesh that speaks and hears itself speaking in the absence of the world. The phenomenological voice is one of pure reflexivity.

In describing this voice also as breath, Derrida anticipates that it will necessarily prove to be a silent voice. For mere breathing is a condition for vocalization, inspiring, as it does, the air that is made to impact the windpipe; yet it is a condition that itself stops short of producing vocal sound and that must in fact be suppressed as such in order for such sounds to be produced.

In its broader import, Husserl's reduction of speech to the phenomenological voice, to the intention that animates speech, constitutes in the most radical form what Derrida calls phonocentrism. Since it is in the phenomenological voice that presence—that is, being as presence, as self-presence—is preserved, Derrida's description in *Of Grammatology* comes directly to the point: phonocentrism maintains "absolute proximity of voice and being, of voice and the meaning of being, of voice and the ideality of meaning."[10] If *Voice and Phenomenon* is regarded as what comes first in a classical philosophical architecture and even if in a certain way it is submitted to the strange geometry of stapling works in the middle of each other, then in the identification of the phenomenological voice, that is, of phonocentrism, the starting point would have been reached from which to pursue the question of writing. For the more thoroughly speech is internalized as the phenomenological voice, the

---

10. Derrida, *Of Grammatology* (Paris: Les Éditions de Minuit, 1967), 23.

more writing is forced out into an exteriority where it is no more than an image of speech. Yet, it is of utmost importance to observe that Derrida's intent is not simply to invert this order so that the outside would be posited inside and conversely. It is not as though speech and hence the voice would be expelled to mere exteriority and thereby rendered secondary, merely and completely subordinated to writing. The voice—or rather, voices—will not be silenced by deconstruction but rather will be released from silence and allowed again—if ever they have—to sound.

Adherence to Derrida's testimony that *Voice and Phenomenon* would come first in a classical philosophical architecture prescribes that the beginning of this text be considered with utmost care. Its opening move is addressed to Husserl's reduction of speech to the phenomenological voice. Specifically, it repeats deconstructively the series of steps by which Husserl internalizes speech to the point where it becomes simply the circuit of speaking-hearing-oneself-speaking, that is, pure reflexivity. This is the point where speech becomes simply a moment within the self-presence of consciousness.

Without venturing to retrace in detail the various steps of the Husserlian analysis and of Derrida's dismantling of each, let it suffice to observe that with each step, Husserl disengages from the essential core of speech a moment that, were it to remain integral to speech, would install therein opacity, externality, or nonpresence, thus contaminating pure self-presence. To risk a metaphorical description, one might regard Husserl's procedure as one of stripping away all the husks of mere indication so as to reveal the core of pure expression.

The entire procedure is, then, a reduction of indication, of the various forms of indication involved in ordinary communicative speech. Husserl commences by separating off as indicative such features as gestures and indeed all those that involve visibility and spatiality in distinction from the spiritual, animating intention. The step that is perhaps most decisive is the one addressed to the moment of intimation (*Kundgabe*). The intimating function is that by which speech indicates the existence of inner experiences in the speaker. In the case of communication, the meaning-intention of the other person is not present, and consequently what is intimated falls outside the presence definitive of consciousness. Derrida identifies the exact point of the reduction: "The notion of *presence* is the nerve of this demonstration. If communication or intimation is essentially indicative, this is because we have no originary intuition of the presence of the other's lived experience. Whenever the immediate and full presence of the signified is concealed, the signifier will be of an indicative nature."[11]

In order, then, to preserve the core of pure expression, Husserl must demonstrate that when speech remains this side of communication with another, it includes no intimating function. In other words, he must show that there is no intimation operative in speech in solitary mental life. Derrida focuses on what he regards as the most decisive of Husserl's arguments in support of such exclusion. In the First Logical Investigation, Husserl writes: "In a monologue words can perform no function of indicating the existence of mental acts, since such indication there would be quite purposeless. For the acts in question are themselves experienced by us at that very same moment [*im selben Augenblick*]."[12] Husserl's argument is, then, that there is no intimation in solitary speech because there is no need for it, because it would be purposeless, since the mental act that would be intimated is experienced in the same moment. Within the moment, within the present in which words are uttered to oneself, there is no separation between the utterance and the one to whom the utterance is addressed; within the indivisible moment there is no difference, no otherness, no alterity that would need to be bridged by intimation. In Derrida's words, playing on the German *Augenblick*: "The present of self-presence would be as indivisible as the blink of an eye."[13]

Derrida does not address Husserl's argument immediately but first draws out the presupposition on which it is based, a presupposition regarding the constitution of the present and indeed of time as such. As he then prepares the double reading of Husserl's text on time-consciousness that will undermine this presupposition, he states it in still more precise terms: "Self-presence must be produced in the undivided unity of a temporal present so as to have nothing to reveal to itself by the agency of signs."[14]

Without venturing at all into the deconstruction of the phenomenological concept of time and the microreading of Husserl's intricate text that would be required, let it merely be noted in the most general—and of course inadequate—terms that Derrida's primary focus is

---

11. Derrida, *La Voix et le Phénomène*, 43.
12. Edmund Husserl, *Logische Untersuchungen*, zweiter Band, I. Teil (Tübingen: Max Niemeyer, 1968), 36. Cited in *La Voix et le Phénomène*, 54.
13. Derrida, *La Voix et le Phénomène*, 66.
14. Ibid., 67.

on Husserl's demonstration that the present is essentially, constitutively connected to the immediate past by way of the function that Husserl calls retention or primary memory. But since the immediate past is as such not present, even though it is retained, as past, in the present, it follows that the presence of the present is continuously compounded with a nonpresence, namely, that of the retended past. Yet, this entails, in turn, that nonpresence is admitted into the originary sphere of the living present, that there is alterity within this sphere, that the presence of the present is produced through a compounding of presence and nonpresence. In Derrida's words: "As soon as we admit this continuity of the now and the not-now, of perception and nonperception, in the zone of originarity common to originary impression and retention, we admit the other into the self-identity of the *Augenblick*; nonpresence and nonevidence are admitted into the *blink of the instant*. There is a duration to the blink, and it closes the eye."[15] Therefore, the supposition of an undivided presence of the present as expressed in the phrase "*im selben Augenblick*" is undermined, as is, then, also the basis on which Husserl sought to exclude the intimation—and hence this form of indication—from solitary mental life.

There are still other forms of indication that Husserl would have to exclude in order to maintain the pure expressivity of speech as such. Among them is that of the sensible sign, primarily of the articulated sound-complex, the spoken word. The sensible sign is, then, to be distinguished from the acts by which an expression is more than mere words, by which it *means* something. Here there is a distinct echo of Aristotle's analysis of voice, especially his insistence on the moment of meaning. And yet, whereas Aristotle for the most part describes *as interconnected* the various components of voiced speech—sound, its physical production, the agency of the soul, and its signifying power—Husserl is intent on rigorously marking an essential distinction between all that has to do with sound *and* the soul's signifying power. In other words, Husserl's analysis would separate the very moments that Aristotle sought to think together.

There is also another echo of Aristotle's account to be heard in the phenomenological analysis, an echo that likewise is both distinct and yet inverted in relation to the Greek original. It is recognizable in Husserl's turn once again to an analysis of solitary mental life, now for the

---

15. Ibid., 73.

sake of a reduction of the sensible sign. In this case it is strictly a matter of reduction and not simply of exclusion. Husserl contends that in solitary mental life the sensible sign undergoes a kind of reduction: sounding words becomes superfluous, and one speaks to oneself *in silence.* And yet, the question cannot but arise: How can such silent monologue constitute expression? How can there be expression without words? It is at this juncture that an echo of Aristotle becomes audible, for Husserl's answer is that there are indeed words involved but that they are merely imagined, phantasized, rather than actual, really existing words. Husserl writes: "In phantasy [*In der Phantasie*] a spoken or printed word hovers before us [*schwebt uns . . . vor*], though in truth it does not exist at all."[16] *Phantasie* directly transliterates the Greek φαντασία, though a long and complex history lies between them. For Aristotle φαντασία must be involved in the agency of the soul by which air is made to impact the windpipe in a certain way. Thus, φαντασία is engaged in the production of voiced sound, of voice as sound, of sound as voice. For Husserl *Phantasie* is involved precisely when there is speech without sound, when the voice is silent; and then it serves, not to foresee that which the voice will signify, but rather only to provide surrogates for the words that have been silenced.

Thus, in Husserl's analysis the sensible sign, the sounding voice and the voiced sound, is reduced to the silent, phantasized word, and it is only in this form that it remains in the speech of solitary mental life, that is, in the expressivity of the silent phenomenological voice. And yet, quite apart from Derrida's response to this distinction, the question imposes itself: Does the substituting of phantasy words for real words—assuming this distinction can be rigorously maintained—succeed in freeing pure expression from dependence on signs? Do not even phantasy signs threaten to interrupt the pure self-presence of the phenomenological voice? In any case, one consequence is unmistakable: despite Husserl's aim of finding in pure expression the very essence of meaningful—as opposed to indicative—signs, his analysis ends up placing all real signs on the side of indication. In Derrida's words: "We see unmistakably that in the end the need for indications simply means the need for signs. For it is more and more clear that, despite the initial distinction between an indicative sign and an expressive sign, only an indication is truly a

---

16. Husserl, *Logische Untersuchungen*, 36. Cited in *La Voix et le Phénomène*, 49.

sign for Husserl."¹⁷ The attempt to reduce language so as to assimilate it to self-present consciousness simply ends up setting speech completely outside. Consciousness loses its voice, falls silent, and it is only elsewhere, out there beyond, that the sound of voices can be heard.

It is not unthinkable that Husserl might have intervened in the course of Derrida's reduction of indication or indeed that he might have brought forth a determination that would counter the entire reduction. One could imagine Husserl looking over Derrida's shoulder as he writes *Voice and Phenomenon* and repeatedly insisting that Derrida is failing to take full account of the intentional character of consciousness. Husserl would, it seems, have emphasized the radicality of this conception of consciousness: that intentionality is not merely a characteristic belonging to consciousness, that it is not a matter simply of a relation between consciousness and its object, but rather that consciousness is, as such, an opening onto "exteriority" (thereby cancelled *as* exteriority), that it is therefore not a sealed-off interiority, that it is not defined by its solitary mental life but rather, precisely *as* consciousness, exceeds this would-be limit.

In any case and quite apart from such hypothetical intervention, the consequence of Derrida's reduction of indication is explicit: rather than reconciling the self-presence of consciousness with the alterity borne by speech, the analysis has the effect of reaffirming the difference in still stronger terms. The implication, which Derrida will exploit without limits, is that no reconciliation is possible, that speech and the sign in general will always already have contaminated the alleged self-presence of consciousness. Speech will always already have been voiced. The voice will always have sounded at the heart of consciousness—or of what can perhaps no longer be termed consciousness once its self-presence has been disrupted once and for all. Not perhaps without a degree of hyperbole and, in any case, not without more extended and minute analyses than can be retraced here, Derrida will finally declare: "The voice *is* consciousness."¹⁸

From this point on, Derrida's text both leaps ahead ever more rapidly yet also, as if in the same gesture, uncoils a mass of threads by way of the most minute analyses. It is as if the spider were to spin its web in the very act of capturing its prey in the web, yet with little presentiment

---

17. Derrida, *La Voix et le Phénomène*, 46.
18. Ibid., 89.

of what its prey might turn out to be. Let it suffice, then, merely to set out, ever so briefly, a sequence that advances by leaps and bounds from this point on.

In the operation of the voice as the self-affective circuit of speaking-hearing-oneself-speaking, the engendering of self-presence coincides with the installing of difference therein. This production of what Derrida calls "self-relation within self-difference"[19] is not something that happens to a subject, but rather it produces the subject. In other words, it is not as though the subject—or, one could say, consciousness—were already there in advance, already constituted, such that the engendering of self-presence would then take place within it; for the subject is precisely being-present-to-self and comes to be only insofar as presence is engendered. This operation of the voice, this production of the subject, Derrida designates using the neologism différance (with an "*a*"); he calls it the movement of différance. Therefore, the operation of the voice belongs to or even coincides with the movement of différance.

Need it be said? This is another voice, other than the phenomenological voice, other than the voice described by Aristotle, other than most any other in the history of metaphysics.

In Derrida's texts there are many voices. Some occur as citations from Husserl, Heidegger, or other authors. Yet, in the strict sense whatever is set forth in citations is not the voice of another but rather a passage from a written text. Even if what is cited should happen to be words once heard in the voice of another, they will, in being cited, have been transposed into the written text; in this transposition the voice of the other will have been silenced. And yet, we sometimes attest that in reading the words of an author we can hear his voice behind the words, that we can hear it silently resounding.

But the voices in Derrida's texts are by no means limited to citations. On the contrary, a text may include a description of a certain voice or kind of voice. Or, even more directly, certain voices may be identified as speaking in the text, as in a Platonic dialogue, so that the text consists largely or even entirely of speeches uttered by these voices. Nonetheless, as speeches within a text, they are silent; they are not voiced, not at least unless the text is read aloud.

---

19. Ibid., 92.

14   ELEMENTAL DISCOURSES

Among the many texts by Derrida in which voices are prominent—let us call them the vocal texts—there are three that may be mentioned—briefly—as exemplary of three different ways in which voices occur in his texts.

In the first of these texts there are two voices, one of them describing a way in which the other occurs. The first voice is that of Heidegger, and it is set out in the form of a citation from *Being and Time*. The passage cited occurs in the context of a discussion of hearing as belonging constitutively to discourse. Heidegger writes that hearing in the sense of "listening to" is Dasein's way of being open for the other. It even constitutes—so he writes—Dasein's primary way of being open for its ownmost possibilities. Then he adds: "as in hearing the voice of the friend whom every Dasein carries with it."[20] This is the passage that Derrida cites in *Politics of Friendship* and that he interrogated at much greater length in his 1988–89 seminar under the same title. He calls it a "strange and isolated allusion" to this voice. It is indeed isolated in that Heidegger does not elaborate it at all. Derrida brings out what is strange in the passage, namely, that it presents the voice of the friend as "at once both interior and coming from without."[21] Thus, the voice of the friend is both one's own—that is, the condition of it belongs within the orbit of one's self-relation—and yet it is the voice of another, of an irreducible other, a voice that cannot but disrupt the ownness of self-presence, an exorbitant voice. Hence, Derrida's reading—or hearing—of the passage: "It is perhaps in a region thus withdrawn from metaphysical subjectivity that for Heidegger 'the voice of the friend' resounds [*résonne*]."[22]

The second of the vocal texts constitutes the final part of *The Truth in Painting*. This title is a citation from a promise that Cézanne made to Émile Bernard: "I owe you the truth in painting, and I will tell it to you."[23] Both the title and the promise resonate with Heidegger's discourse in *The Origin of the Work of Art*: for Heidegger, what is essential is the truth *in* painting, truth as set into the artwork. What especially interests Derrida is the *owing* that is expressed in the promise. His question is: What does it mean, in relation to painting, to owe something such as truth? What does it mean to keep the promise, to give back what

20. Martin Heidegger, *Sein und Zeit* (Tübingen: Max Niemeyer, 1960), 163.
21. Derrida, *Politiques de l'amitié* (Paris: Galilée, 1994), 269.
22. Ibid., 273.
23. Paul Cézanne, *Correspondance*, ed. John Rewald (Paris: Bernard Grasset, 1937), 277.

is owed, to restitute the truth? It is with the restitution of truth that the final part of Derrida's text deals. The restitution has to do, specifically, with the shoes depicted in the painting by van Gogh that Heidegger discusses in *The Origin of the Work of Art*. The immediate pretext is a paper by Meyer Schapiro, which criticizes Heidegger's discussion of the painting.

Derrida intervenes in the debate between Heidegger and Schapiro by way of what he calls "a polylogue of n + 1 voices," one being that of a woman. The voices are not tied to proper names; they are not attributed to, returned to, identifiable voices; and though it is sometimes evident that certain separate passages come from the same voice, the identity of the voices remains vague. In some cases the comings and goings of these shadowy individuals are revealed: one arrives late; another, the first to speak, who begins with an unmarked citation from Heidegger's discussion, leaves without taking leave and then near the end declares: "I've returned late. I had to leave you on the way. Did someone answer my first question?"[24] At the time he or she posed the question, there were only two people present, not yet, then, a polylogue. The question concerned ghosts in van Gogh's pictures; the word is *fantôme*, but it is soon replaced by *revenant*, which means both *ghost* and *returning*. The ghosts in van Gogh's pictures would return—as ghosts do; they would return what is depicted to the one to whom it is owed.

One of the main points in Schapiro's criticism and in the discussion between the various voices in Derrida's polylogue is whether the van Gogh shoes are those of a peasant woman, as Heidegger maintains, or of a city dweller, even of van Gogh himself, as Schapiro argues. A double restitution is thus at issue: the shoes are to be returned to their owner; and thereby truth, put in question by Schapiro, is to be accorded either to his claim or to Heidegger's. Though the polylogue converges toward restitution of the shoes to the peasant woman and of the truth to Heidegger, there is no unanimity. One voice even continues to find Heidegger's position ridiculous and lamentable. The polylogue does not finally resolve into a monologue. To the end there remain many voices, just as there remain many ways of tying the shoes to the name of the proper owner. As there are many voices in the polylogue, so there are many ghosts in van Gogh's picture.

---

24. Derrida, *La Verité en Peinture* (Paris: Flammarion, 1978), 434.

The third of the vocal texts is *Cinders* (*feu la cendre*). The text proper is again a polylogue, though supplemented on the facing left-hand pages with citations from other texts by Derrida such as *Glas* and *The Postcard*. In the polylogue the voices remain unattributed, as in *The Truth in Painting*. The text proper does not properly begin but rather commences as if it were a continuation of a discussion that the reader does not hear. Both in this retraction of beginning and along the labyrinthine pathways through the text, everything reaches back to the sentence "*il y a là cendre*." If one reads what is written, then the word *là* (with a grave accent) appears as it is, and the sentence translates as "There is cinder there." But if, closing one's eyes, one merely listens to the sentence "*il y a là cendre*," one can readily—perhaps even more readily—hear the word *là* as if it had no accent, hence as a definite article, so that the sentence translates as "There is the cinder" or, more loosely, "Cinders there are." It is this tension between reading and hearing, between writing and speech, that propels the polylogue along its labyrinthine pathway.

In contrast to the polylogical text, the Prologue[25] inscribes only one voice, that of Jacques Derrida, who at the end of the Prologue signs it with his initials. It is, then, the Prologue that describes what is enacted in the polylogue. Derrida writes that the polylogue is "an entanglement of an indeterminate number of voices." He mentions also that the readable grammatical signs that mark voices as masculine or feminine "disappear for the most part when spoken aloud"—like *là* without the accent. Nothing could be less responsive than to attempt to resolve this polylogue into a linear trace of theses or even of questions. But listen to what one voice has to say about cinder—"this thing of which one knows nothing, knows neither what past is still carried in these gray dusty words, nor what substance came to consume itself there before extinguishing itself there"[26] To say it in the idiom of what seems another voice: it is a trace that yet leaves no trace, a trace that is preserved and at the same time lost.[27] Later the word *retrait* (*withdrawal, retreat*) is broached along with the figure of "a pile of cinders unconcerned about preserving its form."[28] Toward the end—which is marked as not an end—there is another voice—if it is another voice—that unmistakably echoes Heidegger, situating cinder in relation to the ontological difference: "I understand

---

25. Derrida, *feu la cendre* (Paris: Des Femmes, 1987), 7–12.
26. Ibid., 25f.
27. See ibid., 17.
28. Ibid., 61.

that the cinder is nothing that can be in the world, nothing that remains as a being [étant]. Rather, it is being that there is [*l'être . . . qu'il y a*]—this is the name of the being that there is there [*qu'il y a là*] but which, giving itself (*es gibt ashes*), is nothing, remains beyond everything that is (*epekeina tes ousias*), remains unpronounceable in order to make saying possible, although it is nothing."[29] Not only is there a proliferation of voices, a polylogue, but also, in this voice, a proliferation of languages. It is as if a single language is insufficient for saying the nothing that makes saying possible, which is also the being that *es gibt*, which also is not only *cendre* but *ashes* (in English), which exceeds all that is, all beings, in a manner comparable to that described at the center of the *Republic*.

In the very title *feu la cendre* the holocaust is invoked, or rather, what could be called holocaust as such, were the *as such* not counter to precisely what would be said in a discourse on the holocaust. Holocaust permeates the polylogue as well as the textual passages cited on the facing pages. Yet it seldom bursts out but rather smoulders beneath what is written in those texts and voiced in the polylogue. One voice calls cinder "what remains without remaining from the holocaust, from the all-burning [*brûle-tout*], from the incineration the incense."[30] Raging beneath the words as well as amidst them, there is fire as the all-burning (ὁλόκαυστον) that consumes even itself, leaving only cinders, ashes, from which nothing arises, no Phoenix. In the words cited from *Glas*, the all-burning "diverges so well from all essential generality that it resembles the pure difference of an absolute accident."[31] In turn, these words converge on the assertion that "the holocaust contains the seeds of ontology [*en puissance d'ontologie*]," that "without the holocaust the dialectical movement and the history of being could not open themselves."[32] The holocaust of the holocaust, as "the irruptive event of the gift," is what "engages the history of being."[33] Yet a voice in the polylogue draws the word back to the event that since the mid-twentieth century it cannot but bring to mind: this voice speaks of a word—one not voiced, perhaps not voiceable—that "would tell of the all-burning,

---

29. Ibid., 57.
30. Ibid., 27.
31. Ibid., 28.
32. Ibid., 30.
33. Ibid., 32.

otherwise called holocaust and the crematory oven, in German in all the Jewish languages of the world."[34]

While it is the tension between the written text and the voiced word that drives the polylogue, a technical supplement to the text allows the indeterminate space between these to be explored in a novel fashion. For along with the text *Cinders*, there was issued a tape recording in which the text is read aloud. To the voices that sound silently in the text, there are added two voices that lend their voices to those in the text. In the alternating readings by Jacques Derrida and Carole Bouquet, the attempt is ventured "to breach a way into the voices at work in a body of writing."[35] The effort is to reveal through the reading voice the potentialities held in reserve by the written text and the capacity of the voice to release the tonal, phonic, and semantic reserves hidden away in the written text. Inasmuch as it is the voice that frees what is merely held in store within writing, it would perhaps not be amiss to mark here in Derrida's vocal enactment a kind of hyper-phonocentrism.

There are—needless to say—many other kinds of voices, some that can be heard in Derrida's texts, others of which only a faint echo is audible. There is the voice of negative theology, a voice that multiplies itself by dividing within itself, speaking in the double voice that says both of two contraries—that God is both without being and beyond being.[36] Then there is the technical voice heard more and more, not only as a human voice recorded and played back but as a voice produced by purely technical means. Since the purely technical voice is entirely devoid of any animating intention, it could be regarded as the diametric opposite of the phenomenological voice. Then there is the musical voice, the voice that ceases merely speaking in order to sing. In the musical voice, tone and speech are blended in a way that renders the musical sound beautiful and installs music among the arts. With musical voices there is no longer polylogue but polyphony.

There are finally—though they are more archaic than final—the voices that are heard in the Platonic dialogues. They are voices that can

34. Ibid., 41.
35. Ibid., 9. Derrida explains: "By entangling itself in impossible choices, the spoken 'recorded' voice makes a reservoir of writing readable, its tonal and phonic drives, the waves (neither cry nor speak) which are knotted in the unique vociferation, the singular range of another voice."
36. See Derrida, "Sauf le nom," 35.

be lent to others as in Socratic ventriloquy. They are voices that sound in such a way that something is also done, a deed accomplished. They are voices that sound from and sometimes blend with mythic tales of gods and heroes—the voice of the blind poet, who tells how Odysseus told of his descent, which opened in advance the way down to the Piraeus. They are voices that can sing, as in the great song of the earth that concludes the protracted and inconclusive discussion on Socrates' last day.

They are voices like that which Socrates the ventriloquist lends to Diotima. Through her words she initiates Socrates into the highest mysteries, leading him along the way that extends from the look of bodies to the beauty of souls and of deeds and finally to beautiful speech and knowledge, which, at once, are speech and knowledge directed to the beautiful. Along this way mythical elements are woven into the discourse, stories such as that of the birth of Eros, who, conceived on the birthday of Aphrodite, becomes her attendant. In relating these stories and, above all, in enacting the ascent—even if not without a downward draft—Diotima would have practiced music making, at least of the kind that Socrates was to undertake in his last days. It is, then, as if her song were echoed and thus confirmed by the sound of the flute girl accompanied by the voice—also disrupting the ascent—of the drunken Alcibiades.

They are voices that, in all these registers, bring something to light, make it manifest, without collapsing into a single voice, into monologue. It is in this capacity above all that the Platonic dialogues remain incomparable.

2 GATHERING LANGUAGE

Language is like imagination. If they are regarded in their most originary character, there appears to be even an inner affinity between them. It is as if each, apart from the other, lets happen something like what comes also to pass with the other.

Imagination is preeminently spectral. It lets an otherwise unseen spectacle be seen. In the classical formulation given in the *Critique of Pure Reason*, imagination is the power of making present something that is not itself present. Imagination enables an event in which something only vaguely intimated is brought to show itself as it determinately is or would be.[1]

It is likewise with language. One speaks or writes, and as one does so, something becomes manifest, something comes to be said in such fashion that it shows itself as what it is. It is not as though, as one begins speaking or writing, one would have in view in its essential determinateness what comes to show itself through the speaking or writing. Rather, it is only in and through the event of speech that it first comes openly into view; it is only as eventuated in and through language that it becomes determinately manifest. What happens in language—provided

---

1. While certain forms of imagination are primarily oriented to vision (one imagines seeing a certain spectacle, sees it in imagination), imagination as such is by no means restricted to visual modes. One can, for instance, imagine hearing a melody, even a melody that one might never actually have heard. For delimiting the most originary forms of imagination, the visual instance does not at all suffice (see *Force of Imagination: The Sense of the Elemental* [Bloomington: Indiana University Press, 2000], chap. 5).

it does not slide toward mere *Gerede*—is therefore never a matter simply of expression.

Speaking can be compounded. We can speak with one another. We can do so, not just to communicate, to transport, a more or less determinate thought from one speaker to another, but in such a way that the disclosiveness of the speaking is enhanced. From Plato to Gadamer it is ever again attested that in dialogue the manifestive power of language can come to exceed what would be possible for each speaker alone.

Yet, it is remarkable that Heidegger ventured to write dialogues. Not many in the history of philosophy have done so, no doubt because the Platonic dialogues loomed over that entire history as paradigms that none could hope to match. It has seemed that in the very first venture into philosophical dialogue the result proved so exemplary that all other efforts were completely overshadowed and appeared only as pale imitations of the Platonic dialogues.

And yet, at what he marks as the end of that history, Heidegger ventures to write dialogues. There are the three dialogues written in the winter of 1944–45 as the Second World War was coming to an end; the third of these dialogues is set in a prisoner of war camp in Russia and thus speaks from out of the extreme historical situation. These three dialogues, collected under the title *Feldweg-Gespräche* and published only in 1995, present invented conversations; it seems that Heidegger planned to extend them, since there are sketches for continuations of all three conversations.[2]

Heidegger's celebrated dialogue with the Japanese is quite different. The text of this dialogue was published in 1959 in *On the Way to Language*. It is the only such text that Heidegger himself published in its entirety; unlike the *Feldweg-Gespräche*, it is a text that he definitely regarded as completed. Heidegger reports that the text originated in 1953–54 and that it was occasioned (*veranlasst*) by a visit by Professor Tezuka from the Imperial University, Tokyo. Heidegger does not describe the text as a transcription of his conversation with Tezuka; indeed, if one compares Heidegger's text with the account that Tezuka published of

---

2. See the Editor's Afterword in Heidegger, *Feldweg-Gespräche*, vol. 77 of *Gesamtausgabe* (Frankfurt a.M.: Vittorio Klostermann, 1995), 246–49. The title *Feldweg-Gespräche* resists translation, especially because of the exceptional sense that *Gespräch* is accorded by Heidegger. The nearest approximation is the title used in Bret Davis's translation: *Country Path Conversations* (Bloomington: Indiana University Press, 2010).

his conversation with Heidegger (which was included with his Japanese translation of Heidegger's text), it is evident that the actual conversation served only as an occasion for an exchange from which Heidegger extracted only some points. Though occasioned by Tezuka's visit and, most likely, by Heidegger's conversations with other Japanese scholars, the actual text is Heidegger's own composition.³

Yet Heidegger does not call these texts dialogues. As with the other three, Heidegger designates the dialogue with the Japanese as a *Gespräch*, deliberately avoiding the word *Dialog*. Although in this connection *Gespräch* is perhaps best rendered as *conversation*, it is imperative to observe that neither the composition nor the semantic range of these two words are perfectly congruent. There is consequently the danger that certain of the tones sounded in the word *Gespräch* will be silenced in the translation. The only way to be assured of avoiding this danger is to let the word remain untranslated. Reticence is also called for with regard to the title that Heidegger gives to his dialogue with the Japanese, the title *"Aus einem Gespräch von der Sprache"*—not only on account of the word *Gespräch* but also because of the polysemy of the preposition *von*, which here can carry any one or more of several meanings, including *from*, *of*, and *on* (in the sense of *about* or *concerning*).

Heidegger's dialogue with the Japanese thus displays a certain singularity. And yet, it incorporates by reference various other dialogues. It begins with recollection of Heidegger's earlier *Gespräche* with Count Shuzo Kuki, who is mentioned repeatedly in the initial exchanges between Heidegger (designated as an inquirer or questioner [*ein Fragender*] and Tezuka (designated as a Japanese). Again and again Heidegger and his interlocutor refer to Kuki's *Gespräche* both with Heidegger and with his own students in Kyoto.⁴ Thus, they launch the current *Gespräch* by weaving it together with a network of others that have

---

3. Observing that Heidegger's text reproduces only very few points from the actual conversation, May concludes that it is "immediately clear that Heidegger has *invented* a challenging dialogue by utilizing a variety of relevant pieces of information and appropriate textual excerpts." He adds: "It is easy to see that the 'Conversation' can be read in large part as a monologue" (Reinhard May, *Heidegger's Hidden Sources: East Asian Influences on His Work*, trans. Graham Parkes [London: Routledge, 1996], 13–15). For Tezuka's account of his conversation with Heidegger, see ibid., 59–64.

4. Though the Japanese speaks of Kuki at the very beginning of the *Gespräch* and often refers to him in the course of the discussion, it is known that in fact Tezuka was not personally acquainted with Kuki but was familiar only with his writings. See May, *Heidegger's Hidden Sources*, 16.

occurred. Furthermore, in the course of the present *Gespräch* they arrange to speak again on the following day: Tezuka will defer his departure in order to visit Heidegger again the next day. A future *Gespräch* that we will not hear is thus protended. Thus, through these interweavings, this evocation and proliferation of other dialogues, the present *Gespräch* places itself within its own discursive temporality. Also, it thereby alludes to its own indefiniteness, its nonclosure.

What is most prominently sounded from the outset of the present *Gespräch* is the danger that threatens every such *Gespräch* between East and West. This danger would have loomed over Kuki's attempts to understand Japanese art by way of European aesthetics as well as over his efforts to convey to Heidegger what is said in the word to which all his reflection was reportedly devoted, the word *Iki*. The danger is first mentioned by the Japanese interlocutor in response to a series of critical questions that Heidegger poses regarding the appropriateness of applying European aesthetic concepts to Japanese art and thought. The Japanese speaks of his sense of the danger of being led astray by the wealth of European concepts to the point where everything genuinely Japanese—the no-play, for example—would be denigrated as indeterminate and amorphous. Heidegger—the Inquirer—responds by declaring that "a far greater danger threatens."[5] Referring back to his *Gespräche* with Count Kuki, he explains: "The danger arose from the *Gespräche* themselves insofar as they were *Gespräche*." The Japanese, in turn, explains that danger threatened because "the language of the *Gespräch* shifted everything into *European*"—whereas, as Heidegger adds, "the *Gespräch* attempted to *say* the essential of *East Asian* art and poetry."[6] Somewhat later the Japanese returns to this point. Again referring back to Heidegger's earlier meetings with Count Kuki, he says: "The language of the *Gespräch* was European; but what was to be experienced and thought was the East Asian essence of Japanese art." In still another formulation, now by Heidegger: "I now see *still* more clearly the danger that the language of our *Gespräch* constantly destroys the possibility of saying that of which we are speaking."[7] Thus, as the *Gespräch* progresses, the danger inherent in just such *Gespräch* comes more and more determinately into view: even greater than the danger of assimilating Japanese art and

---

5. Heidegger, "Aus einem Gespräch von der Sprache," in *Unterwegs zur Sprache*, vol. 12 of *Gesamtausgabe* (Frankfurt a.M.: Vittorio Klostermann, 1985), 84.
6. Ibid., 84f.
7. Ibid., 96, 98.

thought to European aesthetic concepts, in particular, is the danger of assimilating them to European language in general, and of doing so inadvertently in the very launching of a *Gespräch*. Yet, by exposing this danger rather than simply succumbing to it, the present *Gespräch* gains a certain critical edge.

The predicament in which Heidegger's *Gespräche* with his Japanese interlocutors are caught is replicated—though in less extreme form—as we, now, venture a *Gespräch* with Heidegger's German text. An analogous danger threatens as soon as we venture to say in our language what is said in the word *Gespräch*. The primary trait of the word *Gespräch* that prescribes Heidegger's preference for it (rather than the word *Dialog*) consists in its conjoining the prefix *Ge-*, which, as in *Gebirge*, bespeaks a gathering, with a variant form of the very word for language *Sprache*. Thus, the composition of the word calls up, along with its ordinary meaning as conversation, the sense of a gathering of language, even of a gathering of conversation to language. The words *conversation* and *dialogue* do not say what is thus said in the word *Gespräch*. We can elude somewhat the resulting danger by leaving the word untranslated, though it is likely that the danger will reemerge elsewhere on this semantic landscape, perhaps more indirectly and hence in still more dangerous form.

In any case, the danger that haunts—yet also is exposed in—Heidegger's *Gespräch* with the Japanese lies in language. The Japanese gathers up in a few words the entire sounding of the danger: "We recognized that the danger lies in the concealed essence of language."[8] The danger is inseparable from the very power, the hidden power, that language possesses to say that which is addressed, that of which the interlocutors speak. For just as language is capable of saying, it is also capable of not saying, indeed of not-saying in the very event of saying. Thus, within the very disclosure that is accomplished when language lets what is addressed be said, there is—or at least can be—also a leaving unsaid that lets what is addressed remain also in certain respects concealed. In short, the power of language to say and hence to reveal is, at once, a power to withhold saying so as to conceal. Speaking of East Asian art in European language cannot but be exposed to the danger that, in the very disclosure accomplished, it may have concealed something essential. Furthermore, because the saying power of language is hidden, this

---

8. Ibid., 106.

not-saying can remain itself concealed; it may simply go unannounced or it may appear in the deceptive disguise of saying. Then, when it conceals itself, concealment installs itself most obstinately and even to such an extent that the saying power of language can itself remain concealed. In the third of his 1949 Bremen lectures, entitled "The Danger," Heidegger writes: "What is most dangerous in the danger consists in the danger concealing itself as the danger that it is."[9] The danger that lies in the hidden essence of language becomes most dangerous when the essence of language remains itself concealedly concealed and it comes to be taken for granted that language consists of nothing more than signs available to humans for the expression of the meanings entertained by them.

Nonetheless, the danger, recognized as such, must be endured, yet in such a way that the *Gespräch* lets the concealed essence of language be openly operative. In other words, if it is not to remain oblivious to the essence of language, deluded by the concealment of the concealment, the *Gespräch* must proceed in such a way as to let the saying power of language come into play. Indeed at a certain point in the *Gespräch* the Inquirer says that the essence of language "is what is determining our *Gespräch*." Yet, he cautions: "At the same time, however, we must not touch it,"[10] that is, no attempt should be ventured either to submit it to concepts and so to represent it nor even to dispel the concealment that keeps it apart and shelters it from the glare of the demand that it submit to what is called reason.

Inasmuch as the *Gespräch* is determined by the essence of language—*essence* understood in a primarily verbal sense—it exceeds the mere circuit between the two speakers. This exceeding is made explicit in the course of the first of the *Feldweg-Gespräche*. The Guide asks: "And what is the *Gespräch* itself, purely on its own?" He observes, presumably addressing the Scientist: "You evidently don't consider just any mere speaking with one another to be a *Gespräch*." Then he declares: "But it seems to me as though in a proper *Gespräch* an event takes place [*sich . . . ereigne*] wherein something comes to language."[11] In other words, in a proper *Gespräch*—which is not just any speaking together—there

---

9. Heidegger, *Bremer und Freiburger Vorträge*, vol. 79 of *Gesamtausgabe* (Frankfurt a.M.: Vittorio Klostermann, 1994), 54.
10. "Aus einem Gespräch von der Sprache," in *Unterwegs zur Sprache*, 107.
11. Heidegger, *Feldweg-Gespräche*, 56f.

eventuates a coming to language, a saying, that exceeds the mere speech of the interlocutors.

In the *Gespräch* between Heidegger and the Japanese, the interlocutors strive to sustain the reticence needed to hold their speaking open to an eventuation from the essence of language. And indeed they do eventually let be said something belonging uniquely to the Japanese world. It is something already long since said in Japanese, in the word to which Count Kuki had devoted his reflections, the word *Iki*. Thus, what is now ventured is not a saying of something yet unsaid but rather a translation that would gather into a German word that which, uniquely Japanese, has long since been gathered in the word *Iki*. What this word says is now said in German as *das Anmutende*, though various differentiations and qualifications are required to prevent the word from being reabsorbed into the language of European philosophy. Similar measures are needed for the English rendering, *the gracious*.[12]

Much earlier in the *Gespräch*, Heidegger asks the Japanese about the word in his language for what we call language. More precisely, he asks whether there is such a word; if there is not, then how, he asks, does the Japanese experience what we call language? The response by the Japanese hovers between these two alternatives. On the one hand, he attests that he has never before been asked this question and that in the Japanese world no heed has been given to it. This suggests that the word may simply be lacking. And yet, on the other hand, after some moments of silent meditation, he announces that there is such a word. This scene, together with the fact that it is only much later that he actually reveals the word, serves to present dramatically this bringing of language to language. The enactment that is displayed is one of letting the Japanese experience of language be gathered into a word that, though not simply lacking, will only have been intimated as long as this experience has not been drawn into it. Even when Heidegger finally asks him directly about

---

12. Judging from Tezuka's report of his conversation with Heidegger, it seems that they did not speak about *Iki* at all. The translation that is offered, *das Anmutende, the gracious*, has little or nothing to do with *Iki*; the meaning of the word lies, rather, somewhere near the intersection of *elegance, coquetry, refinement, honor, taste*. See Hiroshi Nara, *The Structure of Detachment: The Aesthetic Vision of Kuki Shuzo*, with a translation of *Iki no kōzō* (Honolulu: University of Hawaii Press, 2004). It has been suggested that Heidegger actually confused the sense of *Iki* with that of the word *yūgen*, which can legitimately be translated as *grace*. See May, *Heidegger's Hidden Sources*, 19.

the word, the Japanese hesitates before then saying that it is *Koto ba*. Yet, what the word says, how it says the essence of what we call language, requires a kind of translation that opens onto and reveals its saying power. Drawing together what the Japanese says of *Koto*, Heidegger offers such a translation: *Koto* means "*das Ereignis der lichtenden Botschaft der Anmut.*"[13] This translation borders on the untranslatable, but, with due reservations, let us render it as: the eventuation of a clearing for the arrival of graciousness. The other component, the word *ba*, means petals, as of flowers. The Japanese advises Heidegger to think of cherry blossoms or plum blossoms.[14] Thus, the Japanese word *Koto ba*, which says the Japanese experience of what we call language, can be rendered as: the petals that stem from *Koto*—that is, the blossoming of a clearing in which can arrive the graciousness of what is lovely and luminous.

"That is a wondrous word," exclaims Heidegger.[15] The word can be called wondrous on two accounts. The first is linked to the character of the event in which—as which—the word comes to be spoken in the *Gespräch*. It is an event in which the saying power of language is openly operative as it exceeds the capacities of mere speech. This exceeding is displayed in the *Gespräch* not only by the dramatic moments of meditation and hesitation but, above all, by the translation that commences once the word *Koto ba* has been uttered. Indeed, it is precisely through the translation that it becomes manifest what is said in the word, that is, how the word says what we call language. Even to the Japanese—as he is presented in Heidegger's text—the saying power of the word seems to become more determinately manifest through the translation.

The word can be called wondrous on a second account, for, in the emergence of the word, the saying power of language is brought to bear on language itself, on the essence of language, which is nothing other than this saying power. In the word *Koto ba*, what we call language comes to say itself—that is, the German word *Sprache* comes to be translated as *Koto ba* in a kind of translation that, rather than merely substituting one word for another, is gathered to the saying power of language.

Thus the word *Koto ba* can be said to be wondrous. Here, too, in the word *wundersam* there is a translation, one especially audible to

---

13. "Aus einem Gespräch von der Sprache," in *Unterwegs zur Sprache*, 142.
14. May points out that in Tezuka's report he refers to the word *ba* as meaning, not petals or blossoms, but leaves on a tree (*Heidegger's Hidden Sources*, 19, 60).
15. "Aus einem Gespräch von der Sprache," in *Unterwegs zur Sprache*, 136.

Western ears. The word says what in Greek is called θαυμαστόν. One cannot but wonder whether, in the saying in which language comes to say itself, one arrives at the beginning of philosophy, perhaps even in a sense that exceeds—that is anterior to—the philosophy that, according to Heidegger's declaration, has come to an end.

To the Japanese saying of language as *Koto ba*, Heidegger adds a complementary saying. He remarks that he has himself become hesitant to continue using the word *Sprache* and that he believes he has found a more suitable word, namely, the word *Sage*, which, he explains, means saying in the sense of showing (*Zeigen*). In this saying of language as a saying that shows, it is the disclosiveness of language that becomes prominent, in contrast to the various Western designations, which refer to the act of speaking or to the organs of speech such as the tongue or the voice. Here, too, as with *Koto ba*, there is operative a distinctive translation, namely, *Sage* as *Zeigen*.

Toward the end of the *Gespräch*, the Japanese says: "It seems to me as though, instead of speaking about language, we have now attempted to take some steps along a course that entrusts itself to the essence of saying."[16] His point is that they have forgone speaking about language in a way that would succumb to the danger of turning it into an object. In speaking about language, they have let their speech be gathered to the saying power of language—indeed in such a way that this very saying power comes to be said. Proper speaking—that is, speaking that comes into its own by being gathered to the essence of language—is thus disclosed in the *Gespräch* both through what is said and through what is enacted, both in word and in deed. It is such speaking that is required for a proper *Gespräch*, for a *Ge-spräch*. To shift for a moment to another idiom: Heidegger's dialogue is not only with the Japanese but also with language itself as it deploys its saying power. Heidegger's dialogue is a dialogue with the essence of language.

One name for proper speaking about language is *Besinnung auf die Sprache*—let us say: reflection on language. When the Japanese introduces this phrase, Heidegger extends it by saying that his reflection is "on language in its relation to the essence of Being."[17] This extension serves to connect the discourse of language to the ontological discourse

---

16. Ibid., 154.
17. Ibid., 121.

that in fact is woven into the *Gespräch*. Indeed, this connection between language and Being constitutes one of the primary moments taken up in the *Gespräch*.

In the ontological discourse Heidegger distinguishes, first of all, between two usages of the word *Sein*: it can designate either the Being of beings, that is, the metaphysical sense of Being, *or* Being in its proper sense, that is, the truth of Being, as said in the word *clearing (Lichtung)*.[18] What Heidegger calls the overcoming of metaphysics and describes as a matter of bringing to light the essence of metaphysics so as to set it within its limits prepares the way for the transition from the Being of beings to the truth of Being. Indeed, Heidegger attests that from *Being and Time* on, his concern was to bring Being itself to shine forth. He proceeds to characterize Being itself, Being in its proper sense, as the presencing of what presences (*Anwesen des Anwesenden*) and hence as a twofold (*Zwiefalt*) that is yet a onefold (*Einfalt*). Then, finally and most decisively, he declares: "Accordingly, what prevails in and bears the relation of the human essence to the twofold is language."[19] In other words, it is language that sustains the essential relation of the human to Being itself. It is on the way to language—that is, from language—that humans are granted their relation to Being.

Heidegger's *Gespräch* with the Japanese offers no further elaboration concerning the way in which language sustains the human relation to Being. Yet, at the point in the *Gespräch* where the question arises as to whether, with the wondrous word *Koto ba*, their thinking has come near the source (*Quell*), Heidegger refers explicitly to his 1950 lecture entitled "Language," which, despite his expressed hesitation to let it appear in print, was published in 1959 in *On the Way to Language* along with the *Gespräch* with the Japanese. The reference could not be more pertinent, for this essay, set within the same parameters as the *Gespräch*, addresses the question of the connection between language and Being in an exemplary way; that is, it engages a saying of this relation.

Were we to begin reading the lecture "Language"—here the hypothetical is necessary, since hardly even a beginning can be ventured without the risk of its entirely taking over the present discourse—we would be struck by its opening words: "Humans speak [*Der Mensch*

18. Ibid., 104.
19. Ibid., 116.

spricht]"[20]—especially if we notice how at the end of the lecture, repeating these words, Heidegger then continues: "Humans speak only in that they respond [*entsprechen*] to language. Language speaks [*Die Sprache spricht*]."[21] The lecture moves between these two sayings, displacing human speech in favor of the speaking of language, that is, disclosing human speaking as bound to the saying power of language, as a speaking *from* language. What such a move, such a venture, is said to require concurs entirely with what is prescribed in the *Gespräch* with the Japanese. In the words of the lecture: "To reflect on language thus demands that we enter into the speaking of language in order to take up our stay within language, that is, within *its* speaking, not within ours."[22] It is in the course of making this entry, of carrying out the displacement, that the lecture comes to address the relation between language and Being. Yet, the lecture undertakes to reflect on language *itself*, on language *as* language, not on language as belonging to anything else, as determined by something else. To the question: How does language occur *as* language?—Heidegger answers: Language speaks (*Die Sprache spricht*).

Yet where—Heidegger asks—is the speaking of language to be found? How is its saying power displayed? He answers: it is to be found displayed in *the spoken*, not as a mere residue of speaking but as that in which speaking is gathered and sheltered. Heidegger proposes to attend to something purely spoken, something that harbors an originary or proper speaking. The purely spoken he identifies as the poem. Thus, he turns to Trakl's poem "Ein Winterabend" ("A Winter Evening").

Were we to follow carefully Heidegger's entire reading of this poem, then we could perhaps reenact the listening in which the appeal of these words could be heard, in which one could overhear them calling things forth, summoning things to come closer. But, as a beginning, let us listen to the first stanza:

> Wenn der Schnee ans Fenster fällt,
> Lang die Abendglocke läutet,
> Vielen ist der Tisch bereitet
> Und das Haus ist wohlbestellt.

In translation:

---

20. Heidegger, "Die Sprache," in *Unterwegs zur Sprache*, 9.
21. Ibid., 30.
22. Ibid., 10.

> When the snow is falling by the window,
> Long tolls the evening bell,
> The table is for many laid
> And the house is well provided.

By naming these familiar things that belong to the winter evening (window, snow, bell, house, table), the poem calls them forth. This call is to be heard in the last two lines:

> The table is for many laid
> And the house is well provided.

In calling forth things that sustain and enrich life, the call—says Heidegger—"invites things that they might bear upon men." Yet, in calling them, it also calls the place of those things, the place in which they can have their bearing on the human. Thus, Heidegger writes: "The snowfall brings humans under the sky that is darkening into night. The tolling of the evening bell brings them, as mortals, before the godly. House and table bind mortals to the earth. The things that are named, thus called, gather to themselves sky and earth, the mortals and the godly. The four are originally united in being toward one another. The things let the fourfold of the four stay with them."[23] These four, taken together, Heidegger terms the world. The four delimit the place of things, which, in the speaking of the poem, is called along with—by way of—the calling of things. What the poem calls forth, what its saying power evokes, is the twofold of world and things.

The second stanza begins:

> Mancher auf der Wanderschaft
> Kommt ans Tor auf dunklen Pfaden.

In translation:

> Many who are wandering
> Come to the door on dark paths.

In evoking those who wander on dark paths, the poem calls to those who wander toward death, those who are capable of dying, those who are preeminently *mortal*. Yet, in calling forth mortals, these lines do not directly call the others of the fourfold, do not call forth world. Rather, like the first stanza, they name things: the door, the dark paths. But with the remaining two lines of the stanza, everything changes:

---

23. Ibid., 19.

> Golden blüht der Baum der Gnaden
> Aus der Erde kühlem Saft.

In translation:

> Golden blooms the tree of graces
> Drawing up the earth's cool dew.

These lines expressly call forth the fourfold; the entire second stanza thus calls world to things, whereas the first calls things to world. And yet, world and things do not simply subsist alongside one another; rather, they interpenetrate (*durchgehen*) one another. Heidegger focuses precisely on the space of this interpenetration, offering three names by which it may be called. In penetrating one another, the two traverse a *between* (*Zwischen*). In this *between* the two are one, are intimate (*innig*), and thus the second name of this space is the *intimacy* (*Innigkeit*) of world and things.[24] The intimacy of world and thing is, however, no fusion but rather requires that the two remain separated (*geschieden*)—hence, the third name: the difference (*der Unter-schied*).

The speaking of language as harbored in the poem, the deployment of its saying power as sheltered in the poet's words, calls forth the twofold of world and things; and, most decisively, it calls these forth in the space where they are between one another, in the space of their intimacy, their difference. As it speaks in the poem, language summons this intimate, yet differentiated, twofold in such a way as to sustain and disclose its bearing on mortals. Thus, through this auditional reflection, Heidegger reveals the power of language to sustain the human relation to the twofold, in which is thought concretely the twofold of Being itself.

This way of thinking Being itself cannot but prompt a number of questions that go largely unaddressed in the lecture and, it seems, in the few other texts that take up this way. In the composition of the fourfold, there is an evident pairing that serves to indicate a certain nonsymmetry among the four moments. There is the one pair, earth and sky. If these are taken in their bearing on the human and yet without metaphorical elaboration, then they must be regarded as belonging to elemental nature; earth and sky are the elements that bound the space of nature, in which virtually all that concerns humans comes to pass. Insofar as

---

24. Referring to Hölderlin, Heidegger characterizes *Innigkeit* as "that which keeps apart things in opposition, thereby at the same time bringing them together" (*Erläuterungen zu Hölderlins Dichtung*, vol. 4 of Gesamtausgabe [Frankfurth a.M.: Vittorio Klostermann, 198], 36).

Being is thought by way of this pair, it can be said to be thought elementally. But then, there is the other pair—if indeed it be a pair: the mortals and the godly. How are these—if at all—engaged in nature and hence suited for a relation of intimacy—or mirror-play—with earth and sky? Can the godly be understood otherwise than mythically? How, then, is the mythical related to elemental nature? And how is it that the mortal, the human, which was previously thought as being-in-the-world, is now regarded as one moment *of* the world? Finally and in much broader perspective, must such thinking of world and things be construed as a concrete way of thinking Being itself? Or is it perhaps a way of thinking that finally leaves behind all questions of Being?—that can, with impunity, abandon the preoccupation with Being?

At the very least, it is imperative to insist that a discourse on the elementals can be rigorously carried out only if it proceeds in a phenomenologically descriptive manner and is taken to bear on the human, not as though the human were a moment within the elemental configuration, but rather as the being who is knowingly submitted to the elemental. For the elemental that lies within the human is not the elementality of nature, even if it is principally in comportment to the elements of nature that humans have their abode in nature.

It goes without saying that there is much more to be heard in Trakl's poem. Were we to follow further Heidegger's reading of the poem and the thinking enacted in that reading, then we might begin to hear the resonances that sound in the namings of the space of world and earth—even if, from other directions, from other soundings, we might venture to dismantle the configuration of the fourfold. In any case, we might then hear also how the call calls each—that is, world and things— to rest, to repose, in the other. To make something rest, to put it into repose, is to still (*das Stillen*). The call that calls the double stilling of world and things can itself then be called the tolling (*das Läuten*). Then, finally, with Heidegger's declaration that *"Language speaks as the tolling of stillness,"*[25] the lecture reaches its apogee—in the sense that Heidegger anticipated when, near the beginning, he said that in hovering over the abyss of language "we fall upward, to a height."[26]

Whether, by entering further into the density of Heidegger's reading of Trakl, we could secure a measure of such height, whether even

---

25. "Die Sprache," in *Unterwegs zur Sprache*, 27.
26. Ibid., 11.

a sense of the direction of such a fall could be engendered—these are questions that must be left open. In any case, in order to give some indication as to how the *Sache* is taken up beyond the limit of the *Gespräch* with the Japanese, we have in the meanwhile wandered far from this *Gespräch*. Let us now return to it in order—but now from another kind of distance—to introduce two final points.

The first concerns the distance that Heidegger appears to take from Plato as regards dialogue. Not only does he adhere to the word *Gespräch* in preference to the word most commonly used for the Platonic dialogues, but also, near the end of the *Gespräch* with the Japanese, he raises the question as to whether Plato's dialogues (*Dialoge*) can be considered *Gespräche* in the proper sense. The context is one in which it has just been agreed that a *Gespräch* must take the form of "*ein entsprechendes Sagen von der Sprache*"—a responsive saying from language, that is, a saying that says in response what has been deployed through the saying power of language. Against the background of this agreement, the Japanese then says: "In this sense, then, even Plato's dialogues [*Dialoge*] would not be *Gespräch*." Heidegger's response is cautious: "I would like to leave the question open and only point out that the kind of *Gespräch* is determined by that from which are addressed those who seemingly are the only speakers, the humans."[27]

But could it be that the Platonic dialogues are more closely akin to Heidegger's *Gespräch* than he might have been prepared to admit? To be sure, if the Platonic dialogues are construed as mere conversations between human speakers, then a thorough differentiation can be justified. And yet, it is by no means the case that only the sayings of human speakers enter into the dialogues. Indeed, it is a saying put forth not by humans but by a god, Apollo, that first sets Socrates on his way as the philosopher he becomes. Still more significantly, when—speaking to his friends on his last day—Socrates tells again about how he became the philosopher he is, he centers his account on what he calls his second sailing, which consisted precisely in having recourse to λόγος. What came to speech in Socratic discourse, what in that discourse was set out in response, what became—in Heidegger's phrase—that from which Socrates was addressed, was λόγος itself, the saying power that the Greeks named in the word λόγος. One could point to further features of the Platonic dialogues that demonstrate an affinity with Heidegger's *Gespräche*: that

---

27. "Aus einem Gespräch von der Sprache," in *Unterwegs zur Sprache*, 143.

they exhibit a coherence of word and deed, enacting in certain ways what they say; and that in and through what is said and done, the dialogues accomplish a showing that exceeds what is simply said, making manifest something that no speech alone could reveal.

But what, then, finally, about imagination? The word *Einbildungskraft* occurs only once in the *Gespräch* with the Japanese. The passage comes near the end, at a point where Heidegger repeats something that the Japanese has already said: that the word *Koto ba* says "Petals that stem from *Koto*." What Heidegger then says hints at an affinity between the saying that issues in this word and the operation of imagination: "Imagination would like to wander away into still unexperienced realms when this word begins its saying." The Japanese responds: "It could wander only if it were let go into mere representing [*Vorstellen*]. But where it wells up as the source of thinking [*als Quell des Denkens*], it seems to me to gather rather than to wander. Kant already had an intimation of something of the sort, as you yourself have shown."[28] The reference is clearly to Heidegger's *Kant and the Problem of Metaphysics*, in which the Kantian schematism is taken as showing that imagination is the common root from which intuition and thought stem and by which they are gathered into the connectedness requisite for the possibility of experience.

In response to this passage, especially to what the Japanese says, we could say once again that language is like imagination: as imagination is the source that empowers thinking, so language deploys its saying power to human speech.

Heidegger does not respond to what the Japanese says about imagination. Yet if we were now to respond, then it would be with a question that is already hinted at in what he says. The question is whether it suffices to restrict the operation of imagination to gathering or whether something like a wandering, even a wandering away beyond, does not belong essentially to it. Already in Kant's discourse on aesthetic ideas, one finds outlined a movement of imagination that not only gathers the aesthetic representation to a concept but also draws it beyond, bearing it beyond both word and concept. The case of translation also bears witness to a wandering or a least a hovering (*Schweben*) of imagination between two languages—as is manifestly displayed in the sayings carried out in the *Gespräch*. Even the thinking or poetizing of the between

---

28. Ibid., 138.

of world and things would appear to draw on an operation in which imagination would not only trace a gathering of world and things but also would accord them their difference by its wandering trace of that difference, not only stilling them but also releasing them into discord, as when things are exposed to the elements, as in the howling fury of a storm. In this case, then, imagination would engage not only the tolling of stillness but also the roar of the tempest.

AFTERWORD

What if one were to forgo speaking about the essence of East Asian art in the absence of an artwork? What if one were to renounce speaking from a distance, even in a speech attuned to the speaking of language? What if in this way one sought to evade or at least defer exposure to the danger of assimilation to European languages? What if one were to stand before a painting, a scroll done mostly in ink, by one of the Chinese masters from the Sung Dynasty? Suppose that one were to remain silent for an indefinitely long time, lingering before the work, letting one's vision be undividedly absorbed in the painting, putting out of mind any inscription on the painting that one might be able to decipher, letting it come into play only much later. Suppose one were to cease thinking about what one would see, even forgetting the one who sees, emptying oneself so that there would remain only one's vision. What if then, once the time, entirely without measure, had passed, had announced its passing, one finally, reticently, ventured some words, not from oneself but from the painting, letting what had been seen govern the transition from image to speech? Would one not then, on fortunate occasions, have come to some understanding of East Asian art, not about what could be deemed its essence, but about the singular work and its capacity to draw to itself, around itself, an exorbitant visibility?

3 THE PLAY OF TRANSLATION

In writing about translation, it will not be easy to keep things from getting tangled. In particular, it will not be easy to keep the discourse itself from getting mixed up with its topic. It will not be easy to produce a discourse capable of remaining simply distinct, completely apart, from what the discourse is about. In other words, it will not be easy to write about translation without getting entangled in translation, without getting caught up in translating translation. For even simply to explain what translation is, to interpret the meaning of the word, is in a sense—in one of the primary senses of the word—to translate. One will not succeed in extricating oneself completely from the intricacies of translation; that is, one will be inescapably drawn into the entanglement of translating translation, even as one also draws away, distancing oneself from this doubling, seeking to disentangle oneself.

The pretense of a discourse on translation that would be uncontaminated by translation cannot, then, be sustained. Forthrightness would dictate acknowledging the entanglement and inscribing the discourse within it.

Yet, even such an inscription will prove incapable of stabilizing the sense of translation, of delimiting it by enframing it within firm limits. Its sense will overreach such would-be limits, and slippage and mutation will set in.

For the most part translation is undertaken without reflection on the structure by which it is determined. One simply goes about translating, directing one's attention to the original expression while weighing various expressions by which it might be translated. Yet, even in this case, a certain understanding of the nature of translation is tacitly operative. But what is fundamentally involved in the transition from an expression to its translation remains unconsidered. One simply focuses on carrying out the transition and producing a translation that can be acknowledged—that will be acknowledged by oneself and others—as being appropriate. Or one might aspire to fashion a translation that exceeds being merely appropriate or that proves to be appropriate to a higher degree.

The transition constitutive of translation is seldom prescribed in advance and in its entirety in such a way that carrying it out would be a mere mechanical process. On the contrary, in most cases there is operative a playfulness—for instance, a wavering between various possibilities, an openness eliciting others, summoning the possible to such an extent that this playfulness shapes the course of the translation, rendering its formation tentative and exploratory rather than simply definitive. As with all sorts of play, the player tends to lose himself in the play, to be taken up into it rather than exercising mastery over it; thus, the very structure of play—and of translation as play—is such that it resists being reduced to a subjective activity in full control, exercising mastery as though all that emerged in the play were merely an object gradually being constituted by the subject. Insofar as it is playful, translation follows a course that is not prescribed; rather, the player must submit to a movement of to-and-fro by which this course is laid out only as it is also being followed. While, to be sure, texts do not translate themselves, neither is translation produced by spontaneous acts of a detached subject. Translating takes place between passive and active, and, if such were intact in modern Western languages, would best be expressed in the middle voice.

The delimitation that was to become the classical concept of translation was first formulated within the orbit of Greek philosophy. To the extent that Western thought remained within this orbit—or at least never entirely escaped it—the classical concept continued to govern the understanding of translation throughout much of the history of philosophy. In order to thematize the classical determination, it will be expedient first of all to identify the specific questions to which the classical concept constitutes a response. Here already, in the transition to these questions and the classical response to them, translation will itself necessarily undergo translation.

To translate something is to convey it across an interval. Such, at least, is the word's most general signification. This signification is itself conveyed—that is, translated—across a certain historical interval by the word's etymology. Its Latin root *translatus* was used as the past participle of *transfero*, to carry or bear across an interval. This word, *transfero*, was in turn the translation of the Greek μεταφέρω—hence the connection, still intact, between translation and metaphor.

One of the specific things that can be conveyed across an interval is meaning, as when the meaning of one word is carried over to another. If the interval is that between two languages, then such conveyance constitutes translation in the ordinary sense of translating something in one language into the words of another language. If, on the other hand, the interval lies within a single language, then translation consists in a transfer of meaning between synonyms. Jakobson calls this intralingual translation, in distinction from interlingual translation, which conveys meaning from one language to another.[1] In this connection there is an opening through which translation would come to coincide with all thinking by which a disclosive move is carried out from one expression to another, as when, for example, the transition is made from the word *object* to the expression *that which stands over against a subject*. By letting the concept of translation extend to this degree, it would be brought to include virtually all movement thoughtfully carried out from one expression to another. In this sense it could, then, be said that thinking is translation.

Translation cannot be separated from measure. If a translation spans the difference between two languages, then the transference across the interval separating the expression in one language from its translation into the other language must be governed by a measure by which it can be determined whether the translation is suitable or not, even whether it can properly be designated as a translation. The measure of a translation is its truth; the measure is, specifically, whether—or to what degree—the translation is *true to* the original, true to the discourse that it is put forth as translating. Yet, what does it mean to be true to a discourse, to a written text or to the spoken word? What does it mean to be *true to* anything? As one can be true to a discourse, thereby producing a good translation, one can also, in quite another context, be true to a friend. Thus, in its most general denotation, to be true to something

---

1. Roman Jakobson, *Language in Literature*, ed. Krystyna Pomorska and Stephen Rudy (Cambridge, MA: Harvard University Press, 1987), 429.

does not simply mean corresponding to it, as the dominant historical determination of truth would prescribe. In being true to a friend, one does not correspond to him (whatever sense—if any at all—correspondence would have in this case), but rather, in a certain specific sense, one responds to him. One is true to a friend by respecting, in word and deed, all that is entailed by the particular—in fact, singular—friendship. To be sure, the truth of a translation requires in some respect that it correspond to the original, that it be like the original. Yet, one cannot but ask: What sense does correspondence have in this case? Correspondence in what respect? How can a linguistic unit in one language (a word, a sentence, etc.) be equivalent to—or at least similar to—a unit in another language? Yet, in whatever manner these questions are resolved, it is imperative to grant that in what are taken as the very best translations there is also an almost ineffable quality akin to the respect belonging to a circle of friendship.

It is to the questions concerning the measure, the truth, of translation that the classical determination of translation responds. This determination is set out in Plato's *Critias*. The various moments of this determination and the full context in which it is developed have been elaborated elsewhere and here need only to be retraced in outline.²

The theme of translation is taken up in the course of a story, told by Critias, about the original Athens of nine thousand years ago in its struggle against the aggression of Atlantis. Critias explains that the story had been handed down originally from Solon, who, in turn, had heard it while traveling in Egypt. In the city of Saïs the story had been preserved in writing, not, however, in Greek, but in the foreign language spoken in that foreign land. Thus, in bringing the story back to Athens, Solon was faced with the problem of translation.

Critias describes how Solon dealt with this problem. The description may be translated as follows: "As Solon was planning to make use of the story in his own poetry, he found, on investigating the force of names, that those Egyptians who had first written them down had translated them into their own voice."³ Solon's recognition that the story had been preserved in translation was the result of his investigation of the force of the names involved. What is the force (δύναμις) of a name, of a word (ὄνομα)? The force of a word lies in its capacity to announce something

---

2. See my *On Translation* (Bloomington: Indiana University Press, 2001), 51–62.
3. Plato, *Critias*, 113a.

or someone, to announce that which it names, thereby making it present in a certain way. This way of making present is to be distinguished from the way in which sense-perception (αἴσθησις) makes present. Because names bring things to presence, thereby rendering them manifest, they are eminently capable, especially when they are preserved in writing, of serving as the repository of memory.

Solon's investigation of the force of the names belonging to the translation of the story would, then, have taken the form of a recovery of their capacity to make manifest and thereby of that which they served to make manifest. Activating the names, putting their force in force, Solon could then carry through the translation into Greek. Thus, Critias' narrative continues: "So he himself, in turn, retrieved the thought [διάνοια] of each name and leading it into our own voice wrote it out."[4]

Here for the first time the basic structure of translation is determined. It is an operation of putting in force the manifestive force of words set in a foreign voice, of doing so in such a way as to retrieve the thought they make manifest, so as then to lead that thought into one's own voice. This inaugural, still proto-classical determination later comes to be stabilized, indeed simplified, into the classical determination, which subsequently will govern, for the most part, the understanding of translation. According to the schema of this determination, translation consists in the movement from an element or expression in one language to a corresponding element or expression in the other language; this movement is carried out by way of circulation through the signification, the meaning. Translation is a circuit running from one language through its meaning to another language in which there is restitution of this meaning. The truth of translation in the sense of correspondence is also determined: a translation corresponds to its original if it has the same meaning. The measure of translation would thus be restitution of meaning.

And yet, is it only the restitution of meaning that provides the measure of translation? Is a translation of a poem—assuming that poetry can be translated—solely a matter of its meaning? Are there not more nearly ineffable elements that are essential to most translations? Not even Cicero, with whom the classical determination has become firmly established, limits translation to the circulation through meaning or thought; rather, he insists that it is also essential that the figures in which the thoughts are expressed also be carried over to the translation of a text.

---

4. Ibid., 113b.

The classical determination of translation remains in force in modernity, indeed throughout most of modernity. Yet, there is expressed again and again a sense that true translation requires more than merely the circulation through meaning, more than the mere restitution of denotation. This sentiment is explicit, for example, in the expressed self-understanding of certain translators of classical works. Among these is Thomas Taylor, who, near the outset of modernity, translated not only the *Timaeus* and the *Critias* but also Proclus' rich and massive commentary on the *Timaeus*. In the latter, Taylor concludes his Introduction with a brief discussion of the translation as such. He writes: "With respect to the following translation, I have only to observe, that I have endeavored to the utmost of my ability to unite in it faithfulness with perspicuity, and to preserve the manner as well as the matter of the original."[5] Here he attests that his translation is guided by two primary concerns. On the one hand, it is meant to be faithful, that is, true to the original. By doing so, he will preserve what he terms the matter of the original, that is, the thoughts, the meanings, as they are woven into the original text and must be rewoven in the production of the translation. In this concern, Taylor reiterates the classical determination in its most direct form. Yet, on the other hand, he is concerned to exercise perspicuity, to discern both what, in particular, faithfulness requires and what needs to be retained beyond the bounds of faithfulness in the strict sense. This excess he designates by the term manner, contrasting it with matter. By manner he means the stylistic and rhetorical elements of the text.

Yet, immediately following his expression of these two concerns, Taylor observes that "the original abounds with errors, not of a trifling, but of the most important nature."[6] These errors, he explains, are of such magnitude that they materially affect the sense, that is, obscure the meaning of the text. His reference of course is not to errors committed by Proclus but those corruptions that have crept into the text as it was handed down and that now abound in what must nonetheless serve as the original from which the translation will have been prepared. Thus, Taylor confesses that he has entered "upwards of eleven hundred *necessary* emendations"—emendations that, he insists, "the sense indubitably demands." By proceeding in this way, Taylor has in effect altered the

---

5. *The Commentaries of Proclus on the Timaeus of Plato*, trans. Thomas Taylor (London, 1820), vii.
6. Ibid.

classical determination of translation: rather than simply circling from the original through the meanings to the translation, he has circled back from the meanings to the original in order to restore the true original; only then does he proceed on the circuit from the restored original through the meanings to the translation. Being true to the original thus acquires a double sense, its restitution regressing from the meaning before then progressing through the meaning to the translation.

Finally, Taylor describes his translation as a gift by which he imparts to others the treasures of ancient wisdom. Yet, it is not a gift meant for everyone; that gift was already bestowed in antiquity in the form of Proclus' original work in the original language. Taylor, on the other hand, imparts this treasure to those who share his native tongue. The gift is beneficent, for it delivers the ancient treasures not only to those who lack the knowledge of the ancient language but also—so it seems—to those who, though capable of reading the original in the original, somehow benefit from reading it in their "native tongue." It is a gift to all who share Taylor's native tongue or who will inherit that tongue in the future. Just as the philosophy of Plato and Aristotle was a good imparted by divinity, so, says Taylor, "I could not confer a more real benefit on the present age and posterity than by a dissemination of it in my native tongue."[7] One could say that Taylor lets Proclus speak English so that he can speak to all who share this native tongue.

The Preface to Alexander Pope's celebrated translation of *The Iliad* begins with invention: "Homer is universally allow'd to have had the greatest *Invention* of any writer whatever."[8] The intent of the word *invention* is not to describe what the poet produces; it is not the poetic work that constitutes *an* invention (as we must say, inserting the article). Pope's reference is simply to invention, not to *an* invention, nor to *the* invention produced by the poet. Neither is it the intent of the word to designate the activity, the productive labor, by which the poet brings forth his work. Rather, *invention* is the name of that which is the antecedent condition by which it first becomes possible to engage in genuinely poetic activity and thereby to produce a truly poetic work. Invention is the gift, itself unaccountable, that allows one to become a great and fruitful poet. Invention is genius or at least is the distinguishing mark of genius.

---

7. Ibid., viii.

8. *The Iliad of Homer*, trans. Alexander Pope (New York: Penguin Books, 1996). All subsequent citations from Pope are taken from the Preface to his translation.

Capitalizing both words, Pope writes that it is "Invention that in different degrees distinguishes all great Genius's."

Pope declares that in his translation he endeavors to show how Homer's vast *Invention* surpasses that of any other poet. This demonstration is to be carried out in all the constituent parts of *The Iliad*. Yet, neither Homer's invention as such, his genius, nor the poetic composition in which he engages can be directly displayed. All that can be displayed in the original and imported into the translation are the effects of his invention, that it makes "his manners more *lively* and *strongly marked*, his speeches more *affecting* and *transported*, his sentiments more *warm* and sublime, his images and descriptions more *full* and *animated*, his expression more *rais'd* and *daring*, and his numbers more *rapid* and *various*." Such are, then, the qualities that attest to Homer's invention, his genius, and these are qualities that must be carried over to the translation if it is to be true to the original. Yet, reference to these qualities provides no hint whatsoever as to how Pope's translation is to carry out the progression that the classical concept considers primary, the circling from original to its meaning and from the meaning to the translation.

However, once Pope turns from the theme of invention and the qualities of the poetic work that springs from it to his treatment of his translation and indeed of translation in general, the question of truth in the strict sense comes into play. The translator, he says, is to avoid "wilful omissions or contractions," so as to present the original "entire and unmaim'd." Yet, such a presentation cannot be a literal translation any more than it can be a paraphrase. Passage from original to translation is necessarily limited, for there are features that cannot literally be carried over along with, as integral to, the meaning, features that are not simply drawn across the semantic interval. These features must be recreated by the translator. Pope mentions two such features, diction and versification, and declares that only these are the "proper province" of the translator.

In the case of diction, there are two characteristics with which the translator of Homer must deal, the compound epithets and the repetitions. Pope observes that many of Homer's compound epithets cannot be rendered in English without violating the purity of the language; there are others that "slide easily of themselves into an *English-compound*" or that—as in the case of *cloud-compelling Jove*—have been sanctioned by poets and as a result are familiar. On the other hand, those irreducibly foreign to English must either be expressed in a single word (if possible) or translated by a circumlocution. As an example of the latter, Pope cites the epithet εἰνοσίφυλλος, which, applied to a mountain, would appear ridiculous if translated literally as *leaf-shaking*, but assumes a majestic form if rendered as: *The lofty mountain shakes his waving woods*. Pope attests that there are many repetitions that are not accommodated to our ear; these are to be placed only where they enhance the beauty of a passage. In properly placing them, the translator shows "his fancy and his judgment."

As to the other feature with which the translator of Homer must deal, versification, Pope has little to say except that Homer created exquisite beauties by "perpetually applying the sound to the sense." Pope is content to attest that he has "endeavor'd at this beauty."

Thus, Pope details the various supplements that the translator must create and install within the translation of the poem, supplements that in the translation replace, make up for, all those features that are not transported along with the meaning, all those features that detach themselves from the meaning and that, so detached, cannot be taken up into a transposition that would carry them over, fully intact, to the translation.

Pope offers, finally, a measure by which to determine the limit beyond which the translator is not to take liberties in rendering the original. He writes: "I know no liberties one ought to take, but those which are necessary for transfusing the spirit of the original, and supporting the poetical style of the translation." What the translator must carry over is not simply the meaning, not the literal meaning, but the spirit that animates the meaning; and then, casting his glance back at the nonsemantic features of the original, he must create within the translation the supplements that replace those features. Pope expresses this measure in a single word: "the *fire* of the Poem is what a translator should principally regard."

Can it be said, then—as has again and again been said—that translation inevitably involves less? In some instances at least, the literal meaning of an expression in the original may not be reproducible in the language into which it is being translated. And yet, if the translator succeeds in carrying over the spirit of the expression, this may well constitute a restitution of the meaning that is superior to any that could be achieved by way of an allegedly literal translation. Even further, there are some instances in which the spirit of a semantic element turns out to be expressed more expansively in the translation than in the original—with the result that there is actually a gain in meaning, not a loss.[9] Yet, no matter how complete the transfer of meaning may be, the nonsemantic features that Pope identifies—most notably, diction and versification—will almost certainly be lost in the translation. But whether this loss simply renders the translation inferior to the original depends on the fancy and judgment of the translator; it depends on whether the supplements that he produces counterbalance what has been lost.

In addition to the supplements identified by Pope, there is another that in many instances is required. Paradoxically it involves a move that, even if the restitution of meaning is perfect, supervenes in such a way as to introduce distortion into the translation—or at least what, according to the classical concept of translation, would constitute distortion. In *Truth and Method*, Gadamer stresses that even if a translation replicates the meaning of the original, it typically has to transpose the meaning into a different context. He writes: "The meaning is to be preserved, but, since it is to be understood in a new language world, it must establish its validity therein in a new way." This transposition Gadamer characterizes as a form of interpretation. He concludes: "Thus every translation is already interpretation."[10] In a later text Gadamer puts it still more radically, emphasizing the distortive effect of the insertion of the translation into another language world. He says: "Every translation is like a betrayal."[11] This formulation indicates that the introduction of interpretation into all translation has the effect of submitting translation to its extreme limitation, at least as long as translation continues to be understood according to the classical determination. Interpretation must come into play in order to establish in a new language world the meaning of the text translated; and yet in adapting it to that new world, the interpretive translation inevitably betrays the meaning of the original. It becomes ever more apparent that full restitution of sense has virtually no sense, and it is in this sense that Gadamer's hermeneutics of translation drives the classical determination on toward the limit at which it begins to unravel completely.

---

9. See *On Translation*, 93–97.

10. Hans-Georg Gadamer, *Wahrheit und Methode*, in vol. 1 of *Gesammelte Werke* (Tübingen: Mohr-Siebeck, 1993), 387–88.

11. Gadamer, "Lesen ist wie Übersetzen (1989)," in vol. 8 of *Gesammelte Werke* (Tübingen: Mohr Siebeck, 1993), 279.

Hegel was quite aware that the world—and hence the language world—of the early nineteenth century differed to an incalculable degree from that of Greece in the classical era. Nonetheless, he was also aware of the enormous force of the words and expressions that were shaped in and through the thought of Plato and Aristotle, such force that their manifestive capacity had largely endured even up to the era of German Idealism. It was this awareness that prompted Hegel to adopt numerous Greek words, translating them into German, into his language world, yet in such a way that, taken in their respective contexts, it is quite transparent that they are direct translations from the Greek.

And yet, with Hegel, it is not just a matter of interpreting these words so as to bring them, in their translated form, into accord with the language world of early nineteenth-century Germany. Rather, it is a matter of a thinking that recovers what was said and thought in these words, that recaptures their force, and that draws this force into the thinking that Hegel undertakes—not, then, just interpretation, perhaps not interpretation at all, but thinking, a thinking that reanimates the Greek words and releases their force.

In the Preface to the second edition of the *Science of Logic*—the *Vorrede*, which is properly a beginning before the beginning—Hegel writes: "The forms of thought are, in the first instance, displayed and stored in human *language*." The reference that he then makes to thinking as that "which distinguished man from the beasts"[12] is indicative that it is the task of thinking to recover its own forms from the language in which they are stored.

Among the Greek words from which, in his thinking, Hegel undertakes to recover, for his thinking, the thinking stored in those words, the following examples may be mentioned: ἐπιστήμη, translated as *Wissen* or *Wissenschaft*; ἄπειρον as *unendlich*; ἐκφαίνω as *scheinen*; ποῖον as *Qualität* or *Bestimmtheit*. In some instances, as with ποῖον, the transposition is mediated by the Latin translation, though for the most part, Hegel's retrieval reaches back to the Greek, not merely to the Latin.

Yet, there are other cases in which it is not a matter of such appropriative translation from the Greek but of fully exploiting the possibilities sheltered within German words. Referring to the many advantages that in a certain respect German has over other modern languages,

---

12. G. W. F. Hegel, *Wissenschaft der Logik*, vol. 1 (Frankfurt a.M.: Suhrkamp, 1969), 19.

Hegel writes: "some of its words even possess the further peculiarity of having not only different but opposite meanings so that one cannot fail to recognize a speculative spirit of the language in them. It can delight a thinker to come across such words."[13] What is called for is to free this speculative spirit so that such opposite meanings can be brought to animate philosophical language as such. Here it would be primarily a matter, not of translation in any classical sense, but of liberation.

It goes without saying that in Hegel's text the most prominent and significant word of this kind is *Aufheben*, so much so that at the end of the first chapter of the *Science of Logic*, Hegel added a Remark explaining this word, interrupting thereby the rigorous advance of the concept. He stresses the importance of the word and observes that it "repeatedly occurs throughout the whole of philosophy." *Aufheben* is distinguished from nothing; that something is *aufgehoben* does not mean that it is reduced to nothing, that is, entirely, once and for all, negated. Since it is a result, it retains a certain determinateness even as it is surpassed. The word has a twofold meaning: "on the one hand, it means to preserve [*aufbewahren*], to maintain [*enthalten*], and equally it also means to let cease [*aufhören lassen*], to put an end to [*ein Ende machen*]." Hegel indicates how the two meanings cohere despite their opposition: "Thus, what is *aufgehoben* is at the same time preserved; it has only lost its immediacy but is not on that account annihilated [*vernichtet*]."[14] In other words, whatever is submitted to an *Aufhebung* is surpassed by the new form that emerges, and yet it is preserved as a moment within this new form.

Aufheben does not yield readily to—it resists, escapes from—efforts to translate it into English. Various alternatives have been tried and of necessity are used in English translations of Hegel's texts—among them, *supersede* and *sublate*. Neither captures the double meaning of *aufheben*. *Supersede* means *to defer, to discontinue, to render void* and thus lacks entirely the meaning *to preserve*. *Sublate* has similarly negative meanings: *to discontinue, to render void, to put a stop to*. *Aufheben* remains untranslated and, as can perhaps now be concluded, is untranslatable. Curiously, however, there has been a kind of recoil in this instance: whereas *sublate* has—etymologically and in terms of past usage—only one of the two meanings of *aufheben*, its persistent use as a substitute

13. Ibid., 20.
14. Ibid., 113f.

for *aufheben* has led to its having—for some ears—the twofold meaning. Here, then, a kind of back-reference to a non-translation has transformed the word into a quasi-translation.

The word's very resistance to translation—in any even remotely classical sense—makes it virtually inevitable that Hegel's thinking, infused and advanced by this word, cannot but, in this instance at least, speak German.

This infusing and advancement of Hegel's thought through the translating—that is, liberation and dissemination—of *aufheben* can be readily observed in the *Phenomenology of Spirit*. Consider, specifically, the beginning of the chapter entitled "The Truth of Self-Certainty." It is in this chapter that the dialectic occurs in which desire, life, and eventually the other self-consciousness emerge. It is here, says Hegel, that we enter the native realm of truth. But what initially is at stake is simply the relation of consciousness to itself, that is, the taking shape of self-consciousness. In its most elementary, immediate form, the relation to self consists simply in the reflection in which the I takes itself as its object. Yet, the emptiness of such a turn of the I to the I is evident: it is one and the same I that is both subject and object, and yet precisely as the I as subject turns to the I as object, precisely in the opening of this difference, the difference between subject and object is cancelled. However, even at this elementary stage, it is not simply a matter of cancellation or negation but also of maintaining, preserving—that is, of *aufheben*. Hegel writes: "but since what it distinguishes from itself is *only itself as* itself, the distinction, as an othering, is immediately *aufgehoben*."[15] While there is here a superseding, a cancelling, of the difference between the I as subject and the I as object, the difference and hence these two sides are also preserved as moments. While the difference is immediate and the *Aufhebung* produces, as Hegel says, "only the motionless tautology of 'I am I,'" the difference remains as precisely that in which mediation will emerge as the dialectic continues. Such mediation takes shape in the following stage of the dialectic. Here self-consciousness is no longer mere reflection on itself but acquires as a second moment a consciousness of something alien, of a sensible-perceptible thing. In its full structure self-consciousness takes shape through the *Aufhebung* of this opposition. In Hegel's words: "In this sphere, self-consciousness presents itself as the movement in which this opposition is *aufgehoben*, and the identity

---

15. Hegel, *Phänomenologie des Geistes* (Hamburg: Felix Meiner, 1952), 134.

of itself with itself becomes explicit for it."[16] Here again, it is not a matter of simply cancelling the difference nor of negating the consciousness belonging to self-consciousness. What is achieved at this stage is precisely the mediation that was lacking at the initial stage, the mediation resulting from the belonging of consciousness to self-consciousness. Consciousness is not simply negated but is also preserved as a moment within self-consciousness. In carrying out the *Aufhebung* of the object of consciousness, self-consciousness becomes *desire*.

To the extent that the word *aufheben* remains virtually untranslatable and, spreading throughout and driving Hegel's thinking—in an enormous and irreducible range of connections and senses—Hegel's thinking retains—even if not with strict necessity—an attachment to the German language. In short, Hegel's thinking cannot but—to this extent—speak German.

This was, quite remarkably, Hegel's ambition. In his letter to Voss, the German translator of Homer, which was drafted at the time when Hegel was writing the *Phenomenology of Spirit*, Hegel describes translation of such classical texts—including also Luther's translation of the Bible—as "the greatest gift that can be made to a people." He explains: "For a people remains barbarian and does not view what is excellent within the range of its acquaintance as its own true property as long as it does not come to know it in its own language. If you will kindly forget these two examples, I may say of my endeavor that I wish to try to teach philosophy to speak German."[17]

And yet, philosophy had already—indeed in its beginning—spoken Greek. Or rather, first of all—as Heraclitus attests—there was listening: οὐκ ἐμοῦ, ἀλλὰ τοῦ λόγου ἀκούσαντας ὁμολογεῖν σοφόν ἐστιν ἓν πάντα εἶναι. In the conventional translation—every word of which must be put in question: "Listening not to me but to the λόγος, it is wise to agree that all things are one."[18] Many, so Heraclitus observes, do not listen. Or, as he writes: "Having heard without comprehension, they are like the deaf; this saying bears witness to them: present they are absent."[19] Many remain uncomprehending, do not understand that "everything happens

---

16. Ibid., 135.
17. *Briefe von und an Hegel*, ed. J. Hoffmeister, vol. 1 (Hamburg: Felix Meiner, 1969), 100.
18. Heraclitus, Fragment B50.
19. Heraclitus, Fragment B34.

κατὰ τὸν λόγον,[20] that all happenings amidst that which is, are already there in the λόγος, like thoughts that are stored in language. This inherence is set forth in the words ἓν πάντα, which are to be said in a saying that is a saying the same, ὁμολογεῖν. Yet it all comes back to listening, not to anyone, but only to the λόγος, and saying the same as what one hears, silently declaring that it is σοφός to say the same. To say in words what has been heard, to give voice to it, to let its silence sound forth, cannot but be, in the most originary sense, translation.

---

20. Heraclitus, Fragment B1

4 THINGS OF SENSE

What if there were no such thing as the body? What if there is indeed no such thing? What if *there is* were reversible into *is there*, and the *there*, along with *being there*, were put in question, rendered open to question, set in proximity to the open, installed in an opening in which nothing would open, an originary opening? What if the deed of the *indeed* were just this opening, a deed performed by no one, since the opening—one might suspect—would not be an opening of anything, nor an opening within an otherwise closed-off space, but rather an opening that would be, at once, the opening of the very space in which it would open? What if that which has always been called the body were in no sense a thing that would be in the manner that things are? What if *the* body did not exist? What if it were irreducibly singular and proper, always an owned body, one's own body, the body of the very one owning it, both owner and owned? How could there be or not be such a thing that would be no thing? What if the body were nothing?

Do these hypotheticals have a bearing on the semantic poverty that the body has suffered? For unlike its apparent opposite, to which it is also, nonetheless, in immeasurable proximity, it has few names. It is as if it were the embodiment of a tautology. It is nearly always called the same, as if it were always just the same, equipped only to transmit sensory messages to its superior. It would be little more than a mute servant conveying, along multiple disparate channels, that which it received but to which it added nothing. All productivity would belong to its superior. What if it could touch nothing but were compelled to leave to its superior all engagement with the things gathered in the surrounding world?

Merleau-Ponty's project aims at countering all that is attested by the semantic poverty of the body. The intent is to liberate the body, to free it from its mute, uncontested servitude, to entice it to touch the things surrounding it. To that end, it must be brought to share the power previously reserved for its would-be superior. It must be shown to be a living and lived body and not just an underpinning for the multiply-named power that has consistently been alleged to command it.

The decisive move toward such a demonstration is announced in the thesis of the primacy of perception. This thesis is directly expressed in connection with the address that Merleau-Ponty gave to the Société française de philosophie shortly after the publication of the *Phenomenology of Perception*. He could not have stated it more succinctly: "THE PERCEIVED WORLD is the always presupposed foundation of all rationality, all value, and all existence. This thesis does not destroy either rationality or the absolute. It only tries to bring them down to earth." Another statement in the address orients the thesis somewhat differently: "By these words, the 'primacy of perception,' we mean that the experience of perception is our presence at the moment when things, truths, values are constituted for us; that perception is a nascent *logos*."[1]

How is it, then, that in perception, by virtue of its primacy, a *logos* emerges, a *logos* that, as nascent, is irreducible to pure intelligibility but that, precisely as *logos*, is equally irreducible to mere sense? It is as correlative to this *logos* that Merleau-Ponty redetermines the fundamental constitution of the body. Executed by means of a variety of phenomenological descriptions and reports of psychological cases, his analysis identifies two primary determinations, which, if not exhaustive, encompass or at least link up with the various other determinations that his research brings to light. The first determination is already broached in *The Structure of Behavior*. Announcing that "the notions of soul and of body must be relativized," he continues: "The body in general is an ensemble of paths already traced, of powers already constituted."[2] A citation from Hegel restates the sense of this determination: "'The moments that the spirit seems to have behind it are also borne in its present depths.'"[3] In varying respects this determination is renewed again and again in the *Phenomenology of Perception* and is stated perhaps most

---

1. Maurice Merleau-Ponty, *The Primacy of Perception* (Evanston: Northwestern University Press, 1964), 13, 25.
2. Maurice Merleau-Ponty, *La Structure du Comportment* (Paris: Presses Universitaires de France, 1967), 227.
3. Ibid., 224.

succinctly in these words: "our body . . . is an ensemble of lived-through meanings [*significations vécues*]."⁴ It is in and as the body that everything sedimented from past experience—such as habits formed long ago—are carried along. These are the meanings and powers that are drawn up from their depth and thus activated in perceptual experience. Merleau-Ponty writes that "if one perceives with his body, then the body is a natural self [*un moi naturel*] and is like the subject of perception."⁵ This is, then, the second determination: the body is the primary subject of perception. In perception its resources are necessarily called up, and consciousness—its concept correspondingly redetermined—cannot but take up these resources.

There is, then, no such thing as the body—not, at least, if it is construed as purely objective. There is no such thing as the body if it were to be denied all productivity and conceived as a mere receptor of sense.

Merleau-Ponty's redetermination of the body as the anchor of perceptual experience prompts in turn, a renewal of inquiry regarding the character of the world as experienced. He writes: "we shall need to reawaken our experience of the world as it appears to us insofar as we are in the world [*nous sommes au monde*] through our body and insofar as we perceive the world with our body."⁶ It is in this connection that, in the *Phenomenology of Perception*, Merleau-Ponty undertakes to reverse, to dismantle, the objectification that has been carried out with ever greater intensity by modern science and philosophy. This objectification extends a propensity already inherent in perception. It lies in our tendency to lose ourselves in the objects of experience, to be captivated by them, to such a degree that we lose sight of the experience itself by which these come to be objects for us. Merleau-Ponty's intent is to bring to light the pre-objective dimension of lived perceptual experience within which we first have access to things; it is this dimension that is unknowingly presupposed by objective thought, which is its second-order expression.

For this undertaking, it is imperative to chart a withdrawal of the body from the objective world. Both *The Structure of Behavior* and *Phenomenology of Perception* put forth demonstrations that the body cannot

---

4. Maurice Merleau-Ponty, *Phénoménologie de la Perception* (Paris: Gallimard, 1945), 179.
5. Ibid., 239.
6. Ibid.

be properly conceived as a mere thing, as the mere seat of various causal processes. The result is a retrieval of the phenomenal body, of the body as lived, of the subjectivized body, of the body as capable of being the subject of perception. This recovery of the phenomenal body has two major consequences. The first bears directly on the difference between consciousness and the body: by subjectivizing the body, Merleau-Ponty renders consciousness radically incarnate. In particular, the perceptual subject is no longer to be regarded as a transcendental subject aloof from the world, as a subject that constitutes the world by merely imposing form on formless, meaningless sense-material received by the body. Rather, the perceptual subject, as bodily, is a subject that inheres in the world, that is saturated with its object. This perceptual subject represents an anonymous, pre-personal level beneath that of our personal, volitional life. This mutation of the subject effects the relativizing of the notions of soul and body that was called for in *The Structure of Behavior*: the soul, that is, consciousness, is reinstalled in the world, and the body is subjectivized, is reconceived as perceptual subject. Thus, the difference between soul and body is not merely mediated but decisively breached.

The second consequence concerns the objects of perception. By withdrawing the body from the objective world, Merleau-Ponty's analysis also withdraws the things to which the body is intentionally connected. Beneath objects in the scientific sense, this analysis uncovers the genuine perceptual things with their gaps, ambiguity, indeterminacy, and dependence on context. The task that Merleau-Ponty undertakes is to exhibit the character of the perceptual dimension as a whole, to show how it is that the perceptual subject and perceived things form a whole or a system. In other words, his problem becomes one of synthesis. What is required is to exhibit the synthesis by which subject and things are conjoined so as to constitute a holistic structure. As regards specifically the body, the task is to display the synthesis by which the subject is always already present to and engaged with objects, the synthesis by which the bodily subject is other than a mere receptor of sensations or of profiles or even of properties of things.

Merleau-Ponty emphasizes that this synthesis is not a process carried out by consciousness. Rather, it is a bodily synthesis, a synthesis of which the body is the agent. And yet, it is not as though Merleau-Ponty simply transfers to the body the synthetic activity previously ascribed to consciousness; the body is not an agent of synthesis that remains aloof from that which it synthesizes, that merely imposes form on a pre-given material. Rather, the body is saturated with its objects to such a degree that it is impossible to distinguish between a form imposed by the body and a material that would be merely given. The body responds to the way it is addressed by things, and the synthesis is one carried out in an exchange.

Merleau-Ponty's analysis of this synthesis is undertaken in the *Phenomenology of Perception*, specifically, in the chapter entitled "The Thing and the Natural World." In this analysis, Merleau-Ponty traces the series of reductions by which, through an analysis spurred on, if covertly, by a natural propensity, the perceptual object comes step-by-step to be dissolved into an aggregate of mere sensations; his strategy is then to counter this reduction by bringing to light the successive moments of the synthesis by which the integrity of the object is restored. The reduction could be regarded as a transcending of the limit of experience carried out in reverse; Merleau-Ponty's counterstrategy would then consist in exposing it as a kind of transcendental illusion.

Merleau-Ponty's account of the reduction begins at its point of inception, at the point defined by the natural attitude: "Here is a die; let us consider it as it is presented in the natural attitude to a subject who has never asked about perception and who lives among things. The die is there, lying in the world. When the subject moves around it, there appear, not *signs*, but sides of the die. He does not perceive projections or even profiles of the die, but he sees the die itself at one time from this side, at another from that."[7] In the natural attitude one simply lives amidst things without putting these things in question and without casting doubt on one's perception of them. To the subject in the natural attitude, perception is taken as being self-evidently a perception of the object itself, not a perception of some signs from which it would be necessary to make an inferential leap to the object itself. To the one who has never wondered about such matters, the die is simply there.

But as soon as we begin to think about perception, to reflect on its possibility and its expanse, the naïve confidence engendered by the natural attitude dissipates. Then we cease merely living in things and find ourselves compelled to take ourselves as perceiving subjects into

---

7. Ibid., 374.

account. We begin to have reservations about what is seen, and as a result we are readily drawn into a series of reductive moves that strip away from the object layers previously taken for granted. The integrity of the object is compromised, indeed disrupted. In Merleau-Ponty's words: "A series of reductions intervenes from the moment we take the perceiving subject into account."[8] First of all, I observe that the die is only something *for me*, that perhaps others nearby do not see it or see it as looking quite different from the way it appears to me. Thus, it ceases to be in-itself and becomes merely a pole of my perceptual experience. Then, secondly, I notice that in fact I observe the die only through sight and hence apprehend only its outer surface. Now the die loses its density, its materiality, and becomes merely a visual spectacle. All that I really see are properties such as size, shape, and color. But, thirdly, I notice that I do not see the die from all sides simultaneously but only profiles of it correlative to the different perspectives from which it can be seen; in relation to an entirely frontal profile, the other faces of the die appear distorted, some even remaining completely unseen. I no longer observe its cubical shape, which now has splintered into perspectival views. Then, finally, I reflect on the fact that what is actually received from the object, what is registered on my sense organs, are only sensations, which are no longer properties, or even profiles, of the thing but merely modifications of my own body.

Once this point has been reached, how is the perception of the die or of any object to be accounted for? It must be shown that, beginning with the mere sensations, the object is restored, reconstituted. One way in which this recovery of the object can be explained is by supposing that an activity of thought brings the manifold of sensations under its gaze and thereby can carry out an intellectual synthesis capable of molding the sensations into coherent wholes. Yet, Merleau-Ponty rejects outright such an explanation on the grounds that a thing reconstituted in such a manner could never match the thing itself as it is perceived, as it will always already have been perceived within the natural attitude.

Here some reservations are in order. For it is not self-evident that only a fully intellectual synthesis would be capable of effectively assembling the sense elements. There are forms of synthesis in which thought is directive without being the agent of synthesis and in which, accordingly,

---

8. Ibid., 375.

the synthesis is not simply imposed from outside that to which it is applied. Such an alternative is put forth by Kant, as in the passage where he writes: "Synthesis in general, as we will hereafter see, is the mere effect of imagination."[9] Still more pertinent is this passage: "A pure imagination, which grounds all *a priori* knowledge, is a fundamental power of the human soul. . . . The two extremes, namely, sensibility and understanding, must stand in necessary connection with each other through the mediation of this transcendental function of imagination."[10] Thus, for Kant the difference between sense (that is, perception) and understanding (that is, thought) is not breached, each passing over in some degree to the other, but rather mediated through imagination in such a way that each remains intact as such. It is not insignificant that in the *Phenomenology of Perception* there is only one brief reference to imagination; it is more or less dismissive and gives a footnote to Sartre's extremely reductive account of imagination as impoverished by comparison with perception.[11] The possibilities that can be opened up by bringing imagination into the theoretical configuration remain closed off for Merleau-Ponty. There would perhaps have been no more effective way of developing the account of synthesis and, more broadly, of steering a course between idealism and empiricism, a strategy that he adopts throughout much of the *Phenomenology of Perception*.

Merleau-Ponty sets out to account for the synthesis in a way quite different from that of idealism or intellectualism. For him it is a matter of showing that the synthesis that consciousness is otherwise invoked to perform is instead effected within the bodily-perceptual dimension itself—that is, that the body is, *in a sense*, the agent of the synthesis. Yet, everything depends on how this sense is to be understood, specifically that it not be understood as merely transferring the synthetic activity from consciousness to the body. Any such mere transfer would be impossible, since the body is not removed from the material to be synthesized and thus cannot bring that material under its gaze, surveying it with a view to its synthesis. For example, when I run my hand over a rough surface, there is not a series of tactile phenomena that the movement of my hand links together into a perception of the rough surface. Still less are the sensations brought together by a conscious—or at

---

9. Kant, *Kritik der reinen Vernunft*, A78/B103.
10. Ibid., A124.
11. See Merleau-Ponty, *Phénoménologie de la Perception*, 374.

least intellectual—act mediated by the movement of my hand. Rather, my hand is already from the outset paired off with the surface, and its movement is what allows there even to be any tactile phenomena. As Merleau-Ponty explains: "Tactile experience... adheres to the surface of our body; we cannot unfold it before us, and it never quite becomes an object. Correspondingly, as the subject of touch, I cannot flatter myself that I am everywhere and nowhere.... It is not I who touches, it is my body; when I touch, I do not think a manifold but my hands rediscover a certain style."[12] Thus, it is not as though there were discrete elements devoid of synthetic connection and over against them an activity of synthesis. It would be more accurate to say that the synthesis is always already under way within the matter itself. Thus, in this dimension Merleau-Ponty blends form and matter and breaches the difference between consciousness and the body.

Merleau-Ponty's specific account is oriented by the series of reductions leading from the object in itself (the object as it appears to a percipient in the natural attitude) to an aggregate of sensations. The aim is to show that this would-be analysis is an abstraction and that, consequently, no separate synthetic activity needs to be invoked in order to account for the passage through the series. The procedure thus involves beginning with sensations and retracing the constitution of the object, showing how at each stage there is already a synthesis under way; hence, it will be shown how each stage leads to the next without any extrinsic synthetic activity having to be called upon. The effect will be to undo entirely the reduction of the object, that is, to restore the object in its proper integrity.

The initial transition in this restoration of the object leads from mere sensations to sensible profiles that can be taken up perceptually. Here it is a matter of marking the way in which the body, rather than just passively receiving sensations, pairs off with whatever is being sensed. In other words, there are no pure sensations that would require an extrinsic synthetic activity. In what might otherwise be termed sensations, the body is already engaged, and through this engagement there is already a proto-perception. Merleau-Ponty explains: "The sentient and the sensible do not stand in relation to each other as two mutually external terms, and sensation is not an invasion of the sentient by the sensible.

---

12. Ibid., 365.

It is my gaze that subtends color, and the movement of my hand that subtends the object's form.... Apart from the probing of my eye or my hand and before my body synchronizes with it, the sensible is nothing but a vague beckoning."[13]

The second transition toward the restoration of the object concerns profiles. According to the reductive analysis, what is strictly given are only profiles. I see the die from this angle, then from another, and so on. It would seem that a synthetic act would be necessary to unite this manifold of profiles. And yet, as Merleau-Ponty writes: "I do not have one perspectival view, then another, and between them a link brought about by the understanding, but each perspective *merges into* the other [*passe dans l'autre*], and if one can still speak of synthesis, it is a question of a 'transitional synthesis.'"[14]

And yet, it is never merely a passage from one profile to another, as if at each moment I saw only the profile and nothing more. Rather, I see the profile *as* a profile *of* something that can present an indefinite number of other profiles corresponding to other perspectives that I might assume. To this extent, if not yet completely and explicitly, I see the profile as that of an object, and thus the transition from the stage of profiles already to this degree opens toward the object.

In this connection it is appropriate to consider the role that the lateral horizon plays as regards the connection between profiles and the object itself. Any particular profile is always within the scope of a lateral horizon consisting of all the other, presently withdrawn profiles that the object can present; even if portions of the object (for example, the sides of a die) that would be seen frontally from other perspectives are visible, they are necessarily distorted, and as such they belong, not to the present profile, but to the horizon. It indeed belongs to the very sense of a profile that the other possible profiles are implicated in it, referenced by it. One cannot see a profile without also being aware of the other profiles that in their totality constitute the lateral horizon. The question must be posed in view of Merleau-Ponty's account: Is the subjectivized body capable of sustaining the horizon? For it is distinctive of such a horizon that the moments belonging to it are both present and absent: present inasmuch as they link up with the frontal profile yet absent in that they

---

13. Ibid., 244.
14. Ibid., 380.

are withdrawn as such from frontal vision. Even if only Kant's definition is invoked, it is evident that imagination is immeasurably more suited to sustain the horizontal structure than is the body alone, however subjectivized it may be. Kant's definition reads: "Imagination is the power of representing in intuition an object *that is not itself present*."[15] One has only to observe that to represent an object in intuition is to let it appear in and to intuition, to bring it to presence. Imagination has, then, the capacity to make present what is, and remains, absent, yoking together presence and absence, just as the frontally viewed profile is yoked together with those that, while absent, constitute the horizon for the present profile.[16]

The larger effect would be to install imagination at the core of perception, robbing perception of the founding role—especially with respect to imagination—that, from Husserl on, phenomenology has ascribed to it. But then the very sense and assertion of the primacy of perception would be put in question.

According to Merleau-Ponty, the structure of perception is such that it opens in and of itself—and not by means of projection—beyond the stage of profiles. It is as if a profile or series of profiles leads us on to properties, which are no longer perspectival. My perspective on a die does not prevent me from seeing that it is cubical in shape. It is as if perception overruns itself, as if its dynamics drive it on toward what at any stage is implicated.

Yet, properties do not exist in isolation; neither do they appear in singular form. A color is not a free-floating quality independent of other properties and of the thing of which it is the color. The wooly red of a carpet would be quite different if it were not the color of a wooly carpet. Hence, there are not independent properties that would need to be connected by means of synthetic activity. Rather, it is the very nature of properties to be always already connected, so that what a property is, its specific character, is never independent of its relation to other properties. Properties are such that they form a total interconnected system. In Merleau-Ponty's words: "a thing would not have this color had it not also this shape, these tactile properties, this resonance, this odor."[17]

---

15. Kant, *Kritik der reinen Vernunft*, B151.
16. See my analysis in *Force of Imagination: The Sense of the Elemental* (Bloomington: Indiana University Press, 2000), 106–17.
17. Merleau-Ponty, *Phénoménologie de la Perception*, 368.

What, then, is the character of the transition from properties to the object to which they belong? Merleau-Ponty insists that the object is not something posited behind the properties as a unifying substratum. It is not something beyond its properties but rather is that onto which the properties open; it is that which is revealed through them. A color is not an independent quality that it would be necessary to connect to the object by means of an explicit act of synthesis. Stated most succinctly: "A color is never merely a color, but the color of a certain object." Or, again: "Color in living perception is a way into the thing."[18] Or, by analogy: "Perception goes straight to the thing and by-passes the color, just as it is able to fasten upon the expression of a gaze without noting the color of the eyes."[19] How, then, according to Merleau-Ponty, is the object to be understood if it is not a thought-unity behind the properties? He explains that it is something like a unique accent or style immanent in the properties: "The unity of the thing beyond all its fixed properties is not a substratum, a vacant X, an inherent subject, but that unique accent that is to be found in each one of them, that unique manner of existing of which they are a second-order expression."[20]

Merleau-Ponty's descriptions of the manner in which properties belong to the object mark a decisive advance beyond the conception of the object—prominent at least since Locke—as a substratum beneath the properties, as an inaccessible "I know not what" that nonetheless underlies and supports the very properties that hide it from view. For Merleau-Ponty the properties are not mutually isolated but rather occur together in a kind of qualitative proximity to one another. Color, shape, resonance, tactile properties are together in the thing, forming there an interconnected system. There is a corresponding proximity of the properties to the thing; none would be what they are if they were not together also with the object. And yet, there is a moment that is lacking—or at least is minimized—in Merleau-Ponty's account. For whatever its proximity to the properties might be, it must also be set apart from them in order for them to be properties *of* the object; and however closely they may be together in the medium provided by the object, they must also be differentiated from one another. The color and shape of an object may be together with each other and, in their very togetherness, together

18. Ibid., 361.
19. Ibid., 352.
20. Ibid., 368.

also with the object. Yet, there must also be differentiation throughout. While the object is thus, on one side, a *medium* in which there is mutual togetherness, it must, on the other side, also be separated, must be different; and as differentiated it will have withdrawn into itself and become a *one* distinct from the many properties. The object must be both medium and one, and it is precisely in its oscillation between these two poles that it would be constituted as an object.[21]

Even with the passage from the properties to the object, the object remains a correlate of my perception; it remains merely an object-for-me. However, in the full act of perception, the object does not simply present itself as for-me but rather as in-itself. Merleau-Ponty writes: "But still, it is such that the thing presents itself to the one who perceives it as a thing in itself and thus poses the problem of a truthful in-itself-for-us."[22] How, then, does the passage from the object for us to the object as in-itself(-for-us) occur? What is the character by which the transition is accomplished, by which the object is constituted as transcendent? Merleau-Ponty identifies this character as a twofold coherence or even identity. The first moment is a gathering of all the sensible aspects of the object into a coherent whole within which a certain identity prevails. Merleau-Ponty describes this moment in these words: "We now discover the core of reality: a thing is a thing because, whatever it says to us, it says through the very organization of its sensible aspects. The 'real' is that milieu where each moment is not only inseparable from the others but in some way synonymous with them."[23] This account describes still more explicitly the configuration in which the properties are together in the object as medium, that is, as their milieu. The second moment consists in an identity of the unified sensible aspects with the sense or significance (*sens*) of the thing. In Merleau-Ponty's words: "The thing is a kind of being in which the complete definition of one attribute demands that of the subject in its entirety and where consequently the sense [*le sens*] is indistinguishable from the total appearance."[24] Or, again: "The very sense [*le sens même*] of the thing is built up before our eyes, a sense

---

21. See G. W. F. Hegel, *Phänomenologie des Geistes* (Hamburg: Felix Meiner, 1952), 89–102.
22. Merleau-Ponty, *Phénoménologie de la Perception*, 372.
23. Ibid., 373.
24. Ibid.

that no verbal analysis can exhaust and which merges with the exhibition of the thing in its self-evidence."[25]

The thing in itself—the "real"—is thus determined by the way in which its sensible aspects cohere and in and through their configuration display a sense that remains inseparable from their appearance, a sense that is built up in and through our bodily engagement with things of sense. The coherence of sense bestows on things a kind of compactness and an inexhaustibility: "The real lends itself to infinite exploration; it is inexhaustible."[26]

Nothing is more remarkable than the way in which the sense of sense comes to be determined in Merleau-Ponty's recovery of the perceptual object from the dissolution to which it had been submitted. For in recovering the things of sense, he shows how sense arises in their very appearing, how in their configuration sense is already sense. In effect, Merleau-Ponty deconstructs the classical opposition expressed in the double sense of sense: its sense as meaning or concept and as referring to things of sense. What he demonstrates is the virtual identity of sense and sense; thereby he renders superfluous the search repeatedly launched in hopes of discovering passage across this alleged difference. Merleau-Ponty reduces this difference to virtual identity. The linearity of philosophy defined by the search for such passage comes to be replaced by an unlimited proximity of sense to sense.

It is there in the interval corresponding to this proximity that the space of thinking opens. It is opened by no one but only through the dynamic of the sense of sense. It is opened from a place that is not yet a place but only the infinitesimal difference between sense and sense.

Thus it is that there is no such thing as the body. Already in Merleau-Ponty's phenomenological analysis of the body, it is subjectivized—that is, the strict differentiation between body and consciousness is replaced by a schema in which each reaches over, encroaches upon, the other, compromising it, contaminating it. There is, then, no longer anything that can simply be designated as the body, for the body will have proven to be always already also consciousness, soul, spirit.

25. Ibid.
26. Ibid., 374.

Yet, the most decisive move is that in which the virtual identity of sense and sense is established. For it is preeminently in reference to sense in its two senses that the sense of body and of soul has been fundamentally determined. If now the body—or what once would have been called the body—is correlative not to sense (to things of sense) apart from sense (as signification) but rather to sense in proximity to sense, then the body is no more apart from sense as signification than the soul is from the things of sense.

The old body, which was no more than a mute receptor, has died away. The task is now to rethink the human as the mutual overreaching of body and soul. The question is whether to think the human in this way may not, in the end, perhaps even from the beginning, require entirely relinquishing the very sense of body.

5 ARCHAIC NATURE

Nature loves to hide. It longs to wrap itself in its cloak, to enfold it tenderly around itself so that to all who undiscerningly look on, it appears invisible—or rather, does not appear at all, since its invisibility is itself invisible. Its heart belongs to seclusion, which shields it from the prying eyes of humans and the ravenous assault they portend or which holds it in wait for those who would approach it with wonder and grant it its proper reign. Withdrawing into itself, nature resists the strategies that, whatever their ultimate intent, would compel it to enter nakedly into the circle of human cognition, speech, and production.

All things not fabricated by human labor are said to be *by nature*; even if human assistance is required, as in the planting of crops or the breeding of animals, such assistance is merely a means by which to hand production over to nature itself. The word φύσις, which was translated into Latin as *natura*, is etymologically related to the verb φύω, which in its middle-passive form φύομαι means to grow, to spring up, to be born. Whereas natural things do indeed spring up from the soil or else are born and, in both cases, then grow to maturity, the underlying productivity of nature itself goes largely unseen.

Primarily as a result of the elusiveness of seclusive, self-hiding nature, a schema derived from another source, from fabrication, was brought to fill its place. This schema formalizes the pattern operative in the production of artifacts. Things that are produced do not grow of their own accord; they do not spring up as from the soil; neither are they born. Rather, they require a human fabricator, an artisan who has in advance—through memory, imagination, or some other power—a view of the artifact to be produced, a view of it either in its singularity or in some degree of generality. Looking to this paradigm, focusing his mind's eye on it, the artisan then crafts the artifact, molding his material in such a way that it looks like the paradigm.

The schema derived by formalization from this pattern of production is, in its primary—though not its only—modality delimited by the determinations μορφή and ὕλη. Insofar as they are results of formalization of concrete practice, they are not themselves concrete, existing phenomena. In particular, ὕλη is only a formal determination, that is, not something existent. Putting this in its most direct, succinct, and perhaps somewhat hyperbolic form, it can be said that there is no such thing as matter. Once this result is acknowledged, the appeal to materialism becomes—to say the least—questionable. Investigation of the forces and means of production as in various eras they bear on human community will only be stymied by drawing on the abstract concept of matter.

Yet, in Aristotle, with whom these determinations become explicit, they are extended quite beyond the sphere of artisanal production, even beyond that of fabrication in general. The schema of μορφή and ὕλη is extended to all things, not only to those produced by human labor but also to those that are by nature. Furthermore, this schema is not only cast over things of nature (τὰ φύσει ὄντα) but also is projected as constituting the nature itself that governs these things.

In *Physics* B1 Aristotle develops what would become the prototypical analysis of nature. He distinguishes between nature and the things that belong to nature, the things that are said to be by nature. He observes that some believe that nature is the first underlying matter (πρώτη ὑποκειμένη ὕλη) in things that have in themselves an ἀρχή of motion or change, that is, of things that are by nature (φύσει). Others, says Aristotle, regard form (μορφή) as the nature of things, and this determination—φύσις as μορφή—Aristotle declares to be nature in a higher degree than is matter. Thus, an originary nature, identified as μορφή, is installed as the interior origin of natural things, as their ἀρχή, as archaic nature. Yet, what is especially significant in the present context is that these two determinations of ἀρχή are the only ones Aristotle considers. In advance it is presupposed that nature is either matter or form, even though Aristotle educes examples and appeals to the testimony of speech. This schema, which is an abstract determination derived from fabrication, is imposed on the realm of nature. Archaic nature is determined as essentially μορφή, and this determination is, in turn, derived ultimately from the artisanal paradigm, the paradigm of paradigm.

In modern philosophy nature as ἀρχή is dissolved; or rather, it dons its invisible veil, concealing itself at the heart of what nonetheless are called natural things. Almost paradoxically, things that are by nature are granted, while nature itself sinks into oblivion. The realm of nature is flattened out, and its primary determination is identified as extension. With Kant natural things are reduced to appearances; yet this move allows their ἀρχή to be acknowledged, not as nature itself but rather as the *a priori* powers of the subject. This ἀρχή cannot hide itself. In Kant's words: "What reason produces entirely out of itself cannot be concealed."[1] And yet, seemingly unrecognized, the ancient schema still remains, with only the slightest disguise, in effect, namely, in the pairing of *a priori* forms and the sensible material that is to be formed in the constitution of appearances. In the *Critique of Pure Reason*, there remains only the merest trace of nature itself in that Kant distinguishes the material sense of nature as the sum of appearances (that is, primarily of natural things) from the formal sense of nature as consisting, not of the totality of beings, but rather as the connection between their determinations.[2] Though the affinity to the ancient concept of nature is remote, this connection can be thought as a remnant of nature in that archaic sense. In Kant's distinction between the two senses of nature, the ancient distinction between nature itself and natural beings is—if from a distance—reaffirmed.

It is in reference to the entire course of modern Western philosophy from Descartes to Fichte that Schelling puts forth his decisive declaration regarding the continuous oblivion of nature. He writes: "All modern European philosophy since its beginning (with Descartes) has this common defect, that nature does not exist for it and that it lacks a living ground."[3]

The oblivion of nature is nowhere more thoroughly attested than in a passage in Marx's *The German Ideology*, written nearly three decades after Schelling put forth this declaration. In Marx's criticism of Feuerbach's appeal to the sensuous world (in opposition to German Idealism), he maintains that this world—that is, nature—is a product of industry

---

1. I. Kant, *Kritik der reinen Vernunft*, in *Kant's Werke*. Akademie-Textausgabe (Berlin: Walter de Gruyter, 1968), Axx.
2. Ibid., A419/B446.
3. F. W. J. Schelling, *Philosophische Untersuchungen* über *das Wesen der menschlichen Freiheit*, in *Schriften von 1806–1813* (Darmstadt: Wissenschaftliche Buchgesellschaft, 1968), 300.

and commerce, of production as it has developed historically. Referring to Feuerbach, Marx writes: "He does not see how the sensuous world around him is, not a thing given direct from all eternity, remaining ever the same, but the product of industry and of the state of society." Marx supports his thesis by reference to the example of the cherry tree: "The cherry tree, like almost all fruit trees, was, as is well known, only a few centuries ago transplanted by *commerce* into our zone, and therefore only *by* this action of a definite society in a definite age has it become 'sensuous certainty' for Feuerbach."[4] And yet, while granting that the cherry tree may not have remained ever the same, one can hardly not counter Marx's assertion by the simple observation that a cherry tree, even if transplanted, is nonetheless a thing of nature, which sprang up from the earth and which, even if transplanted, continues to grow in the manner proper to such things and indeed, more broadly, proper to all that is by nature.

Schelling's declaration regarding the lack of nature in modern European philosophy—that for it nature does not exist—is put forth in his 1809 work *On the Essence of Human Freedom*. Yet, it is in his work of 1800, *System of Transcendental Idealism*, that the theoretical matrix from which the declaration eventually derives is laid out. In this work Schelling introduces the philosophy of nature as a science parallel to and complimenting Fichte's *Wissenschaftslehre*, which, harking back to Kant, Schelling terms *transcendental philosophy*. Both transcendental philosophy and philosophy of nature are defined by the transition they carry out between the subjective and the objective. What distinguishes the two sciences is the difference in their directionalities: they proceed across the divide in opposite directions. Transcendental philosophy begins with the subjective and demonstrates how the objective arises out of it, that is, how the objective is already contained in the subjective. This demonstration adheres closely to that which Fichte carries out in the *Foundation of the Entire Wissenschaftslehre* (*Grundlage der gesammten Wissenschaftslehre*): beginning with the self-positing I, Fichte shows that this positing of itself is possible only if a not-I—that is, the objective—is also posited. The subjective requires the objective in order to be what it is, and in this sense the objective arises out of the subjective. As a result the objective remains within the compass of the subjective—that

---

4. Karl Marx, *Deutsche Ideologie*, in vol. 2 of *Frühe Schriften* (Darmstadt: Wissenschaftliche Buchgesellschaft, 1975), 57.

is, nature lies within the sphere of the subject. It is produced in a positing intrinsically bound up with the subject's positing of itself. Coming forth from the subject, nature lies within the larger sphere determined entirely by the subject. Succinctly expressed: nature is subordinate to subjectivity. More generally, nature belongs to the sphere of the human.

It is otherwise in the case of the philosophy of nature. It begins with the objective, with nature, and undertakes the transition to the subjective, to what Schelling also designates as intelligence. This transition is carried out by showing how theory can be elicited from nature, that is, by displaying intelligible structures in nature. Natural phenomena will then appear, not merely as the opposite of intelligence, but as structured by concepts, which derive from intelligence. The consummation of this demonstrative process would be, in Schelling's words, "the complete spiritualizing of all natural laws into laws of intuition and thought. The phenomena (the material) must wholly disappear, and only the laws (the forms) remain. Hence it is that the more a lawfulness emerges in nature itself, the more the husk disappears; the phenomena themselves become more spiritual, and at length vanish entirely."[5] In the area of optics, for example, it would be shown—again in the words of Schelling—that the phenomena "are nothing but a geometry whose lines are drawn by light, and this light itself is already of doubtful materiality."[6] At its higher level nature will be found to approximate reflection on itself, which is the very structure of subjectivity, and actually to achieve such reversion into itself at the level of the human.

Schelling's insistence that philosophy of nature be introduced alongside transcendental philosophy became the primary point of contention in the correspondence between Fichte and Schelling immediately following publication of the *System of Transcendental Idealism*. In a letter dated November 15, 1800, Fichte begins by complimenting Schelling on his work but then goes on to write: "I still do not agree with your opposition between transcendental philosophy and philosophy of nature. . . . In my view the thing is not added to consciousness nor consciousness to the thing, but rather both are immediately unified in the I."[7]

---

5. Schelling, *System des transcendentalen Idealismus*, in *Schriften von 1799–1801* (Darmstadt: Wissenschaftliche Buchgesellschaft, 1967), 340f.

6. Ibid., 341.

7. *Fichte-Schelling Briefwechsel* (Frakfurt a.M.: Suhrkamp, 1968), 105.

Less than a year later Schelling published his *Presentation of My System of Philosophy*. The title itself announces that Schelling's intent is to distinguish himself once and for all from Fichte. This aim is explicit when, at the outset of the book, he writes: "Fichte could think idealism in a completely subjective sense, whereas I have thought it in an objective sense."[8] A few months later Fichte sent a highly critical letter to Schelling. With reference to philosophy of nature, he writes: "In this I saw again the old errors. But I hoped that in your scientific labors you would find the right way." Fichte goes on to condemn Schelling's idea of a derivation of intelligence from nature, which is the project of philosophy of nature. He mentions that he has received Schelling's *Presentation of my System of Philosophy* and states openly his objection: "In the Introduction you say some problematic things about *my* idealism." He explains: "The question whether the *Wissenschaftslehre* takes knowing subjectively or objectively makes no sense; for these distinctions are first made within the *Wissenschaftslehre*, not outside it and prior to it."[9] Schelling's reply a few months later openly declares his differences with Fichte. He charges Fichte's concept of nature with being reductive, and regarding Fichte's concept of being, which displays the reductionism, he writes: "For you being means the same thing as reality, even as actuality." Near the end of the letter, he notes that, that very day, a book had "appeared by a very superior head, which has as its title *Difference between the Fichtean and Schellingian Systems of Philosophy*."[10] It would in fact turn out that the difference between Fichte and Schelling was expressed most pointedly yet also most comprehensively by Hegel.

There were critics who charged that the object, posited as the point of departure in Schelling's philosophy of nature, was nothing more than the Kantian thing-in-itself in disguise and that philosophy of nature was therefore nothing more than the dogmatism that Jacobi and others had shown to be at odds with itself. If this had been the case, then philosophy of nature would, as it turns out, have determined the object in such a way as to set it beyond the orbit of subjectivity. Nature would have been freed from containment within the sphere of the human. There would be an originary nature, a nature before nature, an archaic nature.

---

8. Schelling, *Darstellung meines Systems der Philosophie*, in *Schriften von 1801–1804* (Darmstadt: Wissenschaftliche Buchgesellschaft, 1968), 5.
9. *Fichte-Schelling Briefwechsel*, 125f.
10. Ibid., 133, 141.

And yet, conceived in this way, nature would be entirely beyond the reach of the subject. By definition it could not appear but could only be blindly posited behind appearances, behind the nature that appears. From the vantage point of the subject it could signify nothing more than an empty concept, even while continuing to be taken as the source of the sense-material of experience. The inconsistency broached by the assumption that there are things-in-themselves is expressed most succinctly in the celebrated declaration by Jacobi: "Without this assumption I could not enter the [Kantian] system, but with this assumption I could not remain inside it."[11] In the guise of things-in-themselves, nature would increasingly love to hide and indeed would hide; but its hideaway would be absolutely remote, and it could never to the slightest degree be enticed to expose itself and come into the open.

Yet those who accused Schelling of smuggling the thing-in-itself in disguise into his philosophy failed to observe that the object posited at the outset of the philosophy of nature is the same object that in transcendental philosophy is shown to be produced by the self-positing subject. In other words, transcendental philosophy and philosophy of nature not only are complementary but together form a single system. In tracing this system, the philosopher would necessarily circulate between the two complementary sciences, moving from the subject to the object posited by it and then from the object posited simply as such back to the subjectivity that was already contained in it.

Thus, Schelling's philosophy of nature is not at all guilty of what Fichte calls the "old errors," thereby referring no doubt to the assumption that there are things-in-themselves. In philosophy of nature there is no place for things-in-themselves, for a nature absolutely remote from the sphere of the subject, from the reach of humans. The question is whether, this side of the hypothetical things-in-themselves, there is a place where nature would be secured against appropriation by the subject. To be sure, philosophy of nature is introduced as a bulwark against absorption into subjectivity. It allows the object to be posited beyond its mere subjective specter, beyond the double of it that is produced entirely within the sphere of the self-positing subject. And yet, as the philosophy of nature is carried out, the path it traverses is one on which everything

---

11. F. H. Jacobi, "On Transcendental Idealism," in *Kant's Early Critics: The Empirical Critique of the Theoretical Philosophy*, ed. B. Sassen (New York: Cambridge University Press, 2000), 173.

that renders the object objective is dissolved into an intelligibility correlative to intelligence, that is, to the subject. In the end, even the husk of the object vanishes, that is, the object is transposed into intelligibility, and there remains nothing purely objective. The object disappears, transformed into intelligible structures. Thus, in the end, the philosophy of nature demonstrates that the object is no more than subjectivity in disguise. Spectral and reflectional phenomena are nothing but a geometry whose lines are drawn by light, which is not a kind of material but a generative principle in nature. Objective phenomena virtually disappear as they asymptotically approach pure intelligibility. Philosophy of nature is—though in a different way—no less reductive than is transcendental philosophy.

Even if account is taken of the role of transcendental imagination, the result is much the same. Within transcendental philosophy, imagination is identified as the primary motive power by which the object is brought forth in its connection with the self-positing subject. Already with Fichte, this role is accorded to imagination. In Fichte's words: "It is therefore here taught that all reality—*for us* being understood, as it cannot be otherwise understood in a system of transcendental philosophy—is brought forth solely by the imagination."[12] Also in the *System of Transcendental Idealism*, the productivity of imagination is taken to be instrumental. Schelling writes that "nothing is actual without production by imagination."[13] When, in one of his most remarkable statements, he writes that imagination is the only capacity "whereby we are able to think and to couple together even what is contradictory,"[14] the primary reference is to the opposition between the self-positing subject and the posited object.

And yet, despite its rich productivity, imagination operates within the sphere of the subject, and the object as brought forth by imagination remains correlative to the self-positing subject. Even if at another level imagination is determined as the power by which contradictories can be thought, the contradiction is that between subject and object; since it is precisely these contradictories that imagination couples together, the object remains within the transcendental sphere. Its visibility, its presence, is unimpaired, and its containment within the transcendental

---

12. J. G. Fichte, *Grundlage der gesammten Wissenschaftslehre*, in vol. 1 of *Werke* (Berlin: Walter de Gruyter, 1971), 227.
13. Schelling, *System des transcendentalen Idealismus*, 426.
14. Ibid., 626.

periphery remains in force. Not even the productivity of imagination can free it from the hold of the subject. Bound in this way, nature cannot hide itself.

In the philosophy of nature, any role that might be accorded to imagination in the transition from object to subject is left implicit, or perhaps not considered at all. Yet the very discerning of concepts, of intelligible structure, in nature could not be carried out except through the power of imagination. In order to discern these structures, they must, with some degree of determinacy, be anticipated. Furthermore, they must be detached from the natural object and sustained in their difference from this object as they are stripped away. Only imagination has the capacity to effect these necessary operations. Thus, insofar as imagination belongs to the subject, the entire course that defines philosophy of nature remains within the scope of subjectivity. On this path of imaginative discernment and detachment, nature has no place to hide—unless it should turn out that imagination is not a power of the subject, only if, freeing itself from subjectivity, imagination could then open a way beyond, an escape to a site where nature might engage its passion to hide itself.

This is precisely the move Schelling makes nearly a decade later in his work *On the Essence of Human Freedom*.[15] Ironically the charge that he levels at modern philosophy in this work—that nature does not exist for it—can be turned against Schelling's own earlier work. For this charge cannot mean that there is no concept of nature whatsoever in modern philosophy; Spinoza, among others, is an obvious counterexample. It can only mean that there is no concept of nature according to which it escapes the hold of subjectivity or that, in the terms of pre-Kantian thought, transgresses the limit prescribed by the concept of substance. Schelling's philosophy of nature comes closest to breaking this bond but, despite its decisive advance, falls short of achieving this goal.

---

15. In the period of Schelling's absolute idealism, the role of imagination is portrayed in a largely negative way. In *Presentation of My System of Philosophy*, he writes: "It is the nature of philosophy . . . to annul [*aufzuheben*] fully everything that mere imagination [*die blosse Einbildungskraft*] has conflated with reason" (Schelling, *Darstellung meines Systems der Philosophie*, 11). Here there appears to be a full retreat from the much richer concept of imagination found in Fichte and in Schelling's earlier works.

It is only in his work *On the Essence of Human Freedom* that Schelling finally advances to a determination of nature that sets it beyond the circle of subject and object. This projection has as its condition the affirmation of absolute identity. Without simply effacing the circle joining subject and object, Schelling extends without limit the mutual passage between them, thereby establishing their identity. The circle, while retained, is at a higher level attenuated to form what Schelling terms the point of indifference. Nature is determined by its noncoincidence with this point and thereby is projected beyond the circle of subject and object. This determination is expressed without qualification: "Nature in general is thus everything that lies beyond the absolute being of absolute identity."[16] This concept of nature—if it can still be called a concept—is determined through the originary distinction between that which exists and the ground of existence. In this regard ground does not designate a being—in theological terms, God—that grounds all other beings. On the one hand, the ground of the existence of God precedes God, is the condition of his existence. Yet, on the other hand, the ground is not simply set apart from God but lies within God. This ground is also the ground of finite things. In Schelling's words, things have "their ground in that which is in God but *is not God himself*, i.e., in that which is the ground of his existence."[17] Thus, according to this determination, ground withdraws from the orbit of creation in which God and finite beings exist. Indeed there is a double containment: ground is contained in God (yet is not God himself), and God is contained in ground in that it grounds his existence. This containment of God is expressed most succinctly in these words: because ground "is nothing other than the eternal ground of God's existence, it must contain within itself, although sealed off [*verschlossen*], the essence of God as a gleaming spark of life in the darkness of the deep."[18] In man this mutual containment is, in a specific modality, also realized. Man is conceived as the locus where the darkness of ground and the light of the divine come together in their unmediated difference. Schelling writes: "In man is the whole power of the dark principle, and in him, too, the whole force of light. In man are the deepest abyss and the highest heaven, or both centers."[19]

---

16. Schelling, *Philosophische Untersuchungen*, 302.
17. Ibid., 303.
18. Ibid., 305.
19. Ibid., 307.

It is ground, thought in this abyssal way, that Schelling identifies as nature, as initial nature (*die anfängliche Natur*), also as old nature (*die alte Natur*)—that is, as archaic nature. What is perhaps most consequential in this redetermination of nature as abyssal ground is that it frees nature both from the circle of subject and object and from the schema of form and matter. For the distinction between darkness and light, between ground and being, does not coincide with either of the traditional distinctions: nature lies outside the circle of subject and object, and it is neither the form definitive of being nor the matter that would be informed. It is a nature of which the artisan would never have had even the slightest intimation.

Schelling marks a certain affinity between nature as ground and the Platonic χώρα. The χώρα is the third kind (neither intelligible nor sensible) and is anterior to the body and the soul of the cosmos. In other words, the χώρα is the origin from which come the elements that the δημιουργός molds into the cosmos. The suggestion that Schellingean archeology is a kind of echo of the Platonic chorology prompts a circling between these two λόγοι along with an exposing of thinking to the conceptual dismantling that both enact.

And yet, in thinking nature as χώρα, it is imperative not to lose sight of the things that are by nature in order that they, reflected back upon the origin, might draw it into a certain proximity to the human purview and install in it a modicum of concreteness. What is thus required, amidst the loss of nature, is a renewed receptiveness to the natural things and elements amidst which we find ourselves. From the wasteland where nature no longer exists, a renewed sense for all that is natural needs to arise, like the Phoenix reborn from his ashes.

Such a renewal is to be found in a certain strain of American thought. This strain is not that of pragmatism, which all too often has been identified with American philosophy as such. It is rather a development that runs from Emerson to the naturalists of the twentieth century.

Emerson's thought moves simultaneously in two different directions. On the one hand, it assumes a stance akin to that of German Idealism. Traces of Fichte, Schelling, and Hegel are to be found throughout Emerson's essays. On the other hand, there is in these texts an opening to nature in its concreteness, a quiet departure from the divorce between man and nature that runs through much of modern philosophy and even, though transformed, in German Idealism.

These two directions are evident at the very beginning of Emerson's text entitled simply *Nature*. Here Emerson offers two distinctive definitions of nature. The first virtually repeats the concept of nature put forth in early German Idealism: "Strictly speaking, therefore, all that is separate from us, all which Philosophy distinguishes as the NOT ME, that is, both nature and art, all other men and my own body, must be ranked under this name, NATURE."[20] This definition is effective in Emerson's further assertions regarding the dominion of man over nature. He writes: Nature "offers all its kingdoms to man as the raw material which he may mould into what is useful. . . . One after another his victorious thought comes up with and reduces all things, until the world becomes at last only a realized will—the double of the man."[21] Still more succinctly, he writes in the essay "Experience": "Thus inevitably does the universe wear our color, and every object falls successively into the subject itself."[22] These passages virtually constitute a paraphrase of the corresponding part of Fichte's *Wissenschaftslehre*.[23]

---

20. Ralph Waldo Emerson, *The Selected Writings of Ralph Waldo Emerson* (New York: Modern Library, 1950), 4.

21. Ibid., 22.

22. Ibid., 361. In "The Over-soul" he is even more explicit: "the act of seeing and the thing seen, the seer and the spectacle, the subject and the object, are one" (ibid., 262).

23. In "The Transcendentalist" Emerson refers to Jacobi's response to Fichte. He mentions that Jacobi refused "all measure of right and wrong except the determinations of the private spirit" (ibid., 91). He goes on to cite a passage in which Jacobi asserts that faults such as the lie of the dying Desdemona are to be pardoned and that thereby "man exerts the sovereign right which the majesty of his being confers on him," setting "the seal of his divine nature to the grace he accords" (ibid.). The passage comes from Jacobi's 1799 *Open Letter to Fichte*. In this text Jacobi expresses from several different perspectives his opposition to Fichte's *Wissenschaftslehre*. For example: "Since I, after all, consider the consciousness of not knowing as the highest in the human being and the site of this consciousness as the site of the true, inaccessible to science, so I must be pleased with Kant that he preferred to sin against the system than against the majesty of this site. Fichte sins against it, according to my judgment, when he wants to include this site in the area of science" (*Philosophy of German Idealism*, ed. Ernst Behler [New York: Continuum, 1987], 120). It is not entirely clear whether Emerson is referring to Jacobi when he adds that if transcendentalism is identified with extravagance of faith or spiritualism, then "there is no pure Transcendentalist" (Emerson, *Selected Writings*, 92).

On the other hand, Emerson writes of nature in another sense: "*Nature*, in the common sense, refers to essences unchanged by man; space, the air, the river, the leaf."[24] In this regard, he celebrates the beauty of nature, which serves, "not for barren contemplation, but for new creation."[25] He writes also of "a life in harmony with Nature," which "will purge the eyes to understand the text."[26]

To live in harmony with nature is to become like a rose. In the essay "Self-Reliance," Emerson describes what might well be called the self-reliance of roses: that they are simply what they are. He writes: "These roses under my window make no reference to former roses or to better ones; they are for what they are; they exist with God to-day. There is no time to them. There is simply the rose; it is perfect in every moment of its existence." The contrast is with man, who, anticipating and remembering, "does not live in the present." The prospect of human happiness, on the other hand, requires that he become like the rose, that "he too lives with nature in the present, above time."[27]

To live with nature is to open oneself to its beauty and to endure its ferocity.[28] It is to let oneself be engaged with the elemental in nature. The very sense of being is linked to space, light, and time.[29] Emerson writes of a vision prompted "amidst the songs of wood-birds" and of being "cleansed by the elemental light and wind, steeped in the sea of beautiful forms."[30] Not that such engagement can empower a return to beginnings: "Man is a stream whose source is hidden. Our being is descending into us from we know not whence."[31] In Emerson's other text entitled *Nature*, there is an incomparable passage attesting to nature in the common sense and to the human opening to it. He writes:

> At the gates of the forest, the surprised man of the world is forced to leave his city estimates of great and small, wise and foolish. The knapsack of custom falls off his back with the first step he takes into these precincts. Here is sanctity which shames our religion, and reality which discredits our heroes. Here we find Nature to be the

---

24. Emerson, *Selected Writings*, 4.
25. Ibid., 13.
26. Ibid., 20.
27. Ibid., 157.
28. See ibid., 252.
29. See ibid., 155.
30. Ibid., 285f.
31. Ibid., 262.

circumstance which dwarfs every other circumstance, and judges like a god all men that come to her. We have crept out of our close and crowded houses into the night and morning, and we see what majestic beauties daily wrap us in their bosom. How willingly we would . . . suffer nature to intrance us. The tempered light of the woods is like a perpetual morning, and is stimulating and heroic. . . . The incommunicable trees begin to persuade us to live with them, and quit our life of solemn trifles.[32]

Emerson describes the various appearances that nature assumes, the guises and disguises in which it comes to be present to us. He writes: "Nature shows all things formed and bound. The intellect pierces the form, overleaps the wall, detects intrinsic likeness between remote things, and reduces all things into a few principles."[33] Yet, this portrayal of the intellect in its forceful, active capacity is balanced by Emerson's description of it as receptive, as merely opening itself to what is to be disclosed: "Our thinking is a pious reception. . . . We do not determine what we will think. We only open our senses, clear away, as we can, all obstruction from the fact, and suffer the intellect to see."[34] Thus according to these accounts, nature appears as penetrable or even as offering itself to our receptive capacity. On the other hand, Emerson attests that natural things easily slip through our fingers no matter how vigorously we try to grasp them. That nature remains always elusive to us belongs to the human condition. For, as he writes: "Nature does not like to be observed"[35]—or, in positive terms, nature loves to hide.

With Thoreau most of the legacy of German Idealism has disappeared in favor of an opening to nature in the common sense. In his journal he writes of mountains that "break at their summit into granite rocks over which the air beats," and he calls these "terrine temples."[36] In another journal entry he describes a thunderstorm in a manner that could not more aptly attest to his openness and receptivity to nature. In his memorial address, Emerson spoke of how Thoreau, on his "endless walks" made in "every day some new acquaintance with Nature"—such as he expresses in these words: "The almost incessant flashes reveal the

---

32. Ibid., 406f.
33. Ibid., 293.
34. Ibid., 294.
35. Ibid., 345.
36. Henry David Thoreau, *Selected Journals* (New York: New American Library, 1967), 179.

form of the cloud, at least the upper and lower edge of it, but it stretches north and south along the horizon further than we see. Every minute I see the crinkled lightning, intensely bright, dart to earth or forkedly along the cloud. . . . And each time, apparently, it strikes the earth or something on it with terrific violence. We feel the rush of the cool wind while the thunder is yet scarcely audible."[37]

Though already broached in Emerson, what becomes highly conspicuous in Thoreau is the shift toward the elemental in nature: the lightning, the thunder, the air, the earth. This emphasis is extended by such later naturalists as Henry Beston. In *The Outermost House*, which is his account of a solitary year spent on Cape Cod beach, Beston writes about almost everything that can be deemed elemental. Of the "pilgrimages of the sun," he writes: "We lose a great deal, I think, when we lose this sense and feeling for the sun. When all has been said, the adventure of the sun is the great natural drama by which we live, and not to have joy in it and awe of it, not to share in it, is to close a dull door on nature's sustaining and poetic spirit."[38] Beston writes also of the concurrence of the elementals—as in a storm: "With the turn of the tide came fury unbelievable. The great rhythm of its waters now at one with the rhythm of the wind, the ocean rose out of the night to attack the ancient rivalry of earth, hurling breaker after thundering breaker against the long bulwark of the sands."[39]

For all their power, these accounts offer for the most part only tacit renewals of the classical concept of nature as transmuted by Schelling beyond the reach of concepts. In particular, these accounts, including Emerson's more explicitly philosophical analysis, only allude to the ancient distinction between nature and natural things. In a sense this is precisely what is to be expected, since—according to the ancient saying—nature loves to hide, not only from undiscerning looks but even from the keen perceptiveness of philosophical thought. And yet, in these accounts there is operative a distinction that, while it does not reproduce the classical distinction, offers a way in which that distinction can now be folded into another. In all these accounts, even if not explicitly, the modes of elemental nature are in some measure detached from natural things. To this extent the natural elements—lightning, thunder, earth,

---

37. Emerson, *Selected Writings*, 895; Thoreau, *Selected Journals*, 204.
38. Henry Beston, *The Outermost House* (New York: Henry Holt, 1949), 59f.
39. Ibid., 84f.

air, the sun in its daily pilgrimages—can be regarded as constituting nature in distinction from natural things. Rather than being conceived as the interior origin of natural things, rather than being construed as a ground antecedent to being itself, nature as elemental would provide and articulate the very space within which natural things would come to be present. Thus—and this has the utmost import—archaic nature can now—in the now of our own thinking—be determined as the elemental space, as the space of the elementals, as the open expanse for all that is of or by nature.

The elements of nature are hardly less self-concealing than an interior origin or an abyssal ground, though their hiddenness is of a different kind. The earth is perhaps most manifestly hidden, most openly concealed. One cannot survey the earth as a whole, cannot take it in a single gaze. Even if, using present-day means, one beholds it from space, its depth remains still hidden from view no less than when one stands upon it and senses the solid support that it grants. The sky, too, is self-concealing. It has no depth, and as soon as one ascends in search of it, it disappears, as if itself attesting that there is no such thing as the sky, while nonetheless, as one stands firmly on the surface of the earth, it is there above, its blueness shining forth or clouds drifting across it. And so it is with the elements of nature, the elements that, in their various concurrences, spaces, and configurations, always love to hide.

Now taking distance, leaping across both an extended historical distance and vast geographical and cultural distance, distances that are therefore perilous, let me venture to make audible some echoes of the Western concept of nature, echoes antecedent to that which they echo. To turn to ancient Chinese thought is not entirely out of order, especially if, as Van Norden maintains on the basis of the respective characters, the Chinese word for *nature* (*xing*) is etymologically related to a word that means *to be born* (*shēng*).[40] The parallel to the Greek word φύσις and φύω is quite remarkable.

Let it suffice to mention only three very brief passages. The first points to a distinction not unlike the Western distinction between nature and natural things. The passage occurs in the *Book of Chuang Tzu*.

---

40. Bryan W. Van Norden, *Introduction to Classical Chinese Philosophy* (Indianapolis: Hackett, 2011), 75.

In a possible translation it reads: "Everything has its innate nature. . . . Everything under heaven is made as it is by the ways of nature."[41]

The second passage comes from the *Tao Te Ching*. It declares, not merely that everything owes what it is to nature, but that each is drawn back into a return to nature. The passage reads in Ivanhoe's translation:

> The myriad creatures are all in motion!
> I watch as they turn back.
> The teeming multitude of things, each returns home to its root.[42]

This return is not unlike the relation, portrayed in Western thought, between natural things and nature as their ἀρχή.

The final passage—also from the *Tao Te Ching*—says, in a remarkably succinct way, how nature, which is distinct from things in their presence, remains persistently absent—how it hides itself. In Hinton's translation:

> Vacant absence slips inside solid presence.[43]

The hiddenness of nature can be addressed not only in the language of Western philosophy, not only in the more poetic writings of classical Chinese thought, but also in the silent disclosiveness of painting. There is perhaps no other painter in Western art who is more dedicated to this task than Paul Klee. Klee was not only a painter but also a theorist of art, and in his writings and lectures he articulated the aims and methods of his painting. Oriented primarily to nature, he expressed the aim of art—and especially of his painting—in the celebrated dictum: "Art does not reproduce the visible but makes visible."[44] To make visible is to bring to light something otherwise invisible, something hidden. Since nature loves to hide, it is to the hiddenness of nature that Klee's painting is, in this regard, directed—that is, his painting seeks to make visible that which in nature is hidden.

One kind of invisibility that Klee seeks to make visible in his painting is the genesis of natural things, the hidden process by which they come to be. In his words: "One learns to look behind the façade, to get

---

41. *The Book of Chuang Tzu* (New York: Penguin, 1996), 68.
42. *Readings in Classical Chinese Philosophy*, ed. Philip J. Ivanhoe and Bryan W. Van Norden (Indianapolis: Hackett, 2001), 170.
43. Lao Tzu, *Tao Te Ching*, trans. David Hinton (Washington, DC: Counterpoint, 2000), 52.
44. Paul Klee, "Schöpferische Konfession," in *Kunst-Lehre* (Leipzig: Reclam, 1987), 60.

to the root of things. One learns to recognize what flows beneath, learns the prehistory of the visible."[45] In this connection Klee was especially attuned to the genesis that secretly, hiddenly, prepares and leads to the mature appearance of a flowering plant. In paintings such as *Northern Garden in Bloom*, he seeks to make the genesis visible in the blooming. Here the blooming is so profuse that it obscures the plants that are blooming. In other words, the objects, the end results, are made to recede behind the blooming that contributes to their mature appearance. An even more evident example of Klee's technique of making visible the otherwise largely hidden genesis of plants is provided by the watercolor entitled *Wall Plant*. Here one sees the root structure essential to vegetative growth. The plant itself is shown in its articulation into several stages of growth, and thus the course of its genesis is displayed.[46]

In the art of the contemporary painter Cao Jun, there are paintings that, like Klee's, aim at making visible certain forms of genesis in nature. Yet Cao Jun expands the scope beyond the genesis of vegetative life. One such painting is actually entitled *Genesis*. The artist explains that it presents the earth in the genesis that preceded the appearance of humans. Another painting, entitled *Boundless*, likewise presents the earth, but now dispersed into configurations of colors; here it is the source from which erupt what could be taken as water, but also as fire paradoxically paired with the water. The coming forth of these elements is prepared, has its genesis, in the earth.[47]

Thus, natural things are made visible in their genesis, preeminently as they come forth from the elemental source, the earth, but also as they are entwined with all that is elemental in nature. Can it, then, still be declared that philosophy has this defect, that nature does not exist for it? Or can the various disclosures that have here been taken up—by way of such texts as those of Schelling and Emerson, in the gesture toward Classical Chinese thought, and in the works of such painters as Klee and Cao Jun—cast light upon nature itself, a light that nonetheless betrays the darkness into which nature insistently withdraws?

---

45. Klee, *Das bildnerische Denken* (Basel: Schwab, 1971), 69.
46. For images and further discussion of *Northern Garden in Bloom* and *Wall Plant*, see my book *Klee's Mirror* (Albany: State University of New York Press, 2015), 82–86.
47. For images of *Genesis* and *Boundless*, see my exhibition catalog *The Art of Cao Jun: Hymns to Nature* (Boston: McMullen Museum of Art, 2018), 56, 93.

6 ALTERITY AND THE ELEMENTAL

Nature sustains itself not only in proximity to the human world but also in a guise in which it exceeds this world. For Levinas this excess of nature takes place through a return, which he describes as a retreat from being. Its itinerary runs from being's refusal of utter negation to the return of nature in the guise of a phantom, in the elusive form of what Levinas calls the *there is* (*l'il y a*). The appropriation of nature is blocked by the disruption of the dialectical transition from being to nothing. Though freed to return, nature will remain determined by being and will return in the form of an existing without existents, of existence devoid of things that exist. As such, it will no longer be the nature that is shaped and formed within the human world. It will appear strange and alien to the measures that order the human world. In its excess and its otherness, it will prove capable of evoking feelings both of sublimity and of terror.

This thesis regarding the retreat of nature immediately poses a series of questions: If nature, thus returning in the guise of the *there is*, is identified as elemental, how is it to be concretely determined? What is elemental nature? Does it indeed return? Must philosophy return to it by way of being, retracing its return? Or is elemental nature always already there? And is this *there*—if it *is*—identical with the *there is*?

Another series of questions haunts the matrix of Levinas' thought. The questions stem from another thesis, which is most explicitly formulated in *Totality and Infinity*: "And *there is* only man who could be absolutely strange to me [*Et il n'y a que l'homme qui puisse m'être absolument étranger*]."¹ Only man? Only those who are of my kind, even if in a sense of kind that is utterly exorbitant? Only those who call themselves human? Not, then, nature even in its most elemental guise? Not even that elemental nature that is *there*?

The question that returns with the question of nature is that of the absolutely strange. It is the question of another alterity.

In *Time and the Other* Levinas introduces the *there is* by beginning with the Heideggerian distinction between *Sein* and *Seiendes*, reformulating the distinction as that between existing (*exister*) and existent (*existant*).² Even though Levinas mentions that he is not ascribing a specifically existentialist sense to these terms, it should not go unremarked that, even with this qualification, the translation is less innocent, less transparent, than its brief presentation might suggest. Even aside from all the questions that would have to be raised about the role played here by the sedimented opposition between essence and existence, there is another reductive temptation broached by this reformulative translation, one perhaps most evident in the parallel presentation in *Existence and Existents*: in this text the distinction is introduced as that "between the individual, the genus, the collective, God, which are beings [êtres] designated by substantives, and the event or act [*l'événement ou l'acte*] of their existence."³ Though the sense of *événement* could perhaps be oriented toward that of *Ereignis*, any tendency to regard *Sein* as act—even as act of existence—would risk reconstituting those traditional conceptualities with which Heidegger has already broken even in *Being and Time* and thus situating Levinas' entire project within the compass of these conceptualities.

But Levinas' translation of the Heideggerian distinction is indeed meant also to mark a break with Heidegger, with the inseparability of existing and existent that Levinas attributes to Heidegger, though he

---

1. Emmanuel Levinas, *Totalité et Infini: Essai sur L'extériorité* (The Hague: Martinus Nijhoff, 1961), 46.

2. Levinas, *Le Temps et L'autre* (Montepellier: Fata Morgana, 1979), 24. This text first appeared as an article in J. Wahl, *Le Choix, Le Monde, L'Existence* (Grenoble-Paris: Arthaud, 1948).

3. Levinas, *De L'existence à L'existant* (Paris: J. Vrin, 1990), 15. This text originally appeared in 1947. The sections on which I shall focus incorporate Levinas' 1946 article "*Il y a*" (*Deucalion* 1 [1946]: 141–54).

finds this break to be anticipated in Heidegger's discussion of *Geworfenheit*: "It is as if the existent appeared only in an existence that precedes it, as if existence were independent of the existent."⁴ For Levinas it is a question, then, of an existing without existents.

Levinas could have found a still more explicit example of the separability of existing and existents in Heidegger's discourse on the nothing in *What Is Metaphysics?* In this text *the nothing* corresponds to what Levianas terms *existing*; it is, accordingly, "the complete negation of the totality of beings." In Heidegger's analysis it is the mood of anxiety that, in this connection, is decisive. In anxiety we are exposed to "the slipping away of beings" and "brought before the nothing itself."⁵

In his assessment of Heidegger's thought and his description of the relation of his own thought to Heidegger's, Levinas assumes a position that points in two very different directions. In an interview with Philippe Nemo, Levinas characterizes *Being and Time* as "one of the finest books in the history of philosophy." He explains that "in *Being and Time*'s analyses of anxiety, care, and being-toward-death, we witness a sovereign exercise of phenomenology." He insists on the necessity of passing through Heidegger's thought: "I think . . . that one who undertakes to philosophize in the twentieth century cannot not have gone through Heidegger's philosophy, even to escape it. This thought is a great event of our century."⁶

On the other hand, Levinas consistently differentiates his thought from Heidegger's, yet in a manner that for the most part remains questionable when confronted with the Heideggerian texts. For instance, in *Time and the Other* he charges that "all the analyses of *Being and Time* are worked out either for the sake of the impersonality of everyday life or for the sake of solitary Dasein." As a result, says Levinas, "the relation to the other . . . plays no role either in the drama of being or in the existential analytic."⁷ And yet, this charge is reductive; it takes into account only the most general shape of Heidegger's work. One has only to cite the following in order to show that, even if it is not the primary theme

---

4. Levinas, *Le Temps et L'autre*, 25.
5. Martin Heidegger, *Was ist Metaphysik?*, in *Wegmarken*, vol. 9 of *Gesamtausgabe* (Frankfurt: Vittorio Klostermann, 1976), 111f.
6. Levinas, *Éthique et Infini* (Paris: Fayard, 1982), 33, 36, 39f.
7. Levinas, *Le Temps et L'autre*, 18.

of the book and even though Heidegger's response is the inverse of Levinas,' the question of the relation to the other is rigorously developed in *Being and Time*. In Heidegger's words: "It is from the authentic being a self of resoluteness that authentic being-with-one-another first arises."[8]

In the Preface to *Time and the Other*, written thirty years after the work itself, Levinas' position with respect to Heidegger is ambiguous. He writes: "*Time and the Other* presents time not as the ontological horizon of the being of beings [*l'être de l'étants*—Levinas' translation of *das Sein des Seienden*] but as a mode of the *beyond being* [*l'au delà de l'être*], as the relationship of thought to the other."[9] Here again Levinas undertakes to distance himself from Heidegger, now with respect to time: time will not be considered as the ontological horizon of the being of beings, not, therefore, as Heidegger conceives it in *Being and Time*. It is rather to be regarded as a mode of the *beyond being* (*l'au delà de l'être*). The phrase is Levinas' translation of the phrase from Plato's *Republic*: ἐπέκεινα τῆς οὐσίας. What is remarkable is that Heidegger uses this same phrase in describing the goal of his inquiry. He says that the question being taken up is that of "the conditions of the possibility of the understanding of being," conditions that in *Being and Time* are identified as the *ekstases* of temporality. He continues: with this question we "want to do nothing but bring ourselves out of the cave into the light." Then, decisively, he adds: "What we are in search of is the ἐπέκεινα τῆς οὐσίας."[10]

Levinas explains further that time is the relation of thought to the other. Whether even this assertion of identity suffices to differentiate Levinas' thought from Heidegger's is open to question. According to Heidegger's analysis: "*Temporality is the originary 'outside-itself'* ['*Ausser-sich'*] *in and for itself.*"[11] To be outside oneself is to engage an alterity in one's very being. Regardless of whether this conception of alterity corresponds to that which emerges in Levinas' analyses, it cannot be justifiably claimed that Heidegger gives no place to the question of time and alterity.

---

8. Heidegger, *Sein und Zeit* (Tübingen: Max Niemeyer, 1960), 298.
9. Levinas, *Le Temps et L'autre*, 8.
10. Heidegger, *Die Grundprobleme der Phänomenologie*, vol. 24 of *Gesamtausgabe* (Frankfurt: Vittorio Klostermann, 1975), 404.
11. Heidegger, *Sein und Zeit*, 329.

Even with regard to the relation between existing and existents, between *Sein* and *Seiende*, Levinas struggles to differentiate his position from Heidegger's. While granting that in Heidegger there is a distinction between these, he insists that there is no separation between them, that the possibility of an existing without existents would, in Heidegger's view, appear absurd. And yet, here again one has only to cite Heidegger: "The attempt to think being without beings becomes necessary because otherwise, it seems to me, there is no longer any possibility of explicitly bringing into view the being of what *is* today all over the earth."[12]

In order to take up, in his own distinctive way, the question concerning an existing without existents, Levinas calls upon imagination. Omitting all indications as to how imagination is to be construed here, how it is to be, as it were, detached from the complex of determinations it has undergone from Plato on, omitting also all indications regarding the complicity of imagination with the question of being, Levinas simply proposes that we imagine something, or rather, that we imagine—or try to imagine—nothingness. Here is his proposal as he formulates it in *Time and the Other*: "Let us imagine the return of all things, beings and persons, to nothingness. Are we going to encounter pure nothingness? After this imaginary destruction of all things, there remains, not something, but the fact that *there is* [*le fait qu'il y a*]. The absence of all things returns as a presence, as the place where everything has sunk away, as a density of atmosphere, as a plenitude of the void, or as the murmur of silence."[13] Thus, the *there is* is what remains, what returns, when everything is—or is imagined to be—destroyed, negated, reduced to nothingness. It is anonymous and impersonal, neither anyone nor anything, no existent at all, an existing without existents, an existing that returns, that remains, no matter what. And yet, to return is not to remain, except if the return is that of beings returning to nothingness and the remaining is that of nothingness. But it is said explicitly both that the *there is* returns (said doubly in the word *revenant*) and that it is what remains when all things sink away or at least are imagined as sinking away. This twofold character can be regarded as corresponding to two directions from which the *there is* can be thought. If thought from the side of being,

---

12. Heidegger, *Zur Sache des Denkens*, vol. 14 of *Gesamtausgabe* (Frankfurt: Vittorio Klostermann, 2007), 5f.
13. Levinas, *Le Temps et L'autre*, 25f.

then its character is to return in the direction of beings; but if thought from the opposite side, from that of beings, then it is that which remains when, in imagination or otherwise, all beings sink away.

In order to elaborate the characterization of the *there is*, it seems—judging from Levinas' text—that one must conjoin terms that could never be conjoined in reference to a being, to an existent. One must pair opposites, posing contradictions in various registers: absence returns as a presence that is yet absence returned; there is place that, sunk away, gives no place; there is density and yet the lightness of air; there is plenitude and void, the murmur of silence. What returns is not, then, a new being or form of being arising from the ashes of another in a way that would resolve the contradiction by which the previous form would have been consumed. Here there is no question of dialectic but, at most, of the interruption of dialectic, the suspension of *Aufhebung*, a refusal of the determinacy of determinate negation. The *there is* "which returns in the heart of every negation" is no being at all; it is "the spectre, the phantom [*le revenant, le fantôme*]" of being.[14]

Levinas does not hesitate to stress the instability to which thought is exposed in approaching the *there is*. *Existence and Existents* opens with the declaration that the Heideggerian distinction both "imposes itself upon philosophical reflection and with equal facility effaces itself before such reflection."[15] Thought experiences a kind of vertigo in pondering the emptiness of being, of mere existing; it slips imperceptibly from being as being to a being in general, a cause of existence, reenacting that very slippage that Heidegger has undertaken to display as governing the entire history of philosophy.

In *Existence and Existents*, too, Levinas appeals to imagination in order to approach existing without existents. Here, too, he proposes that we imagine the reversion of all beings to nothingness. Here, too, he omits all indications as to how imagination is to be construed, thus leaving undetermined the character of the imaginative enactment that he puts forth as the very means of access to the *there is*. One might suppose that imagination is put in play here because it can enact a negation, a reduction of being, one that could never in fact be fully enacted. One might also wonder whether there comes into play here an intimation

---

14. Levinas, *De L'existence à L'existant*, 100.
15. Ibid., 15.

that imagination, determined otherwise, is such that it has the power—indeed *is* the power—of hovering between opposites and holding them together in their opposition. It would, thus, have the capacity to pair those opposites by which Levinas characterizes the *there is*.

In what Levinas writes about the *there is*, there are sustained references to nature and even to elemental nature. For instance, he notes that no substantive can be affixed to the *there is*, that is, that the *il* of the *il y a* is not a substitute for an unexpressed noun but rather simply an impersonal form, as in such expressions as "it rains" or "it is hot."[16] Night is even more pertinent to the *there is*: "If the term experience were not inapplicable to a situation that involves the total exclusion of light, we could say that night is the experience itself of the *there is*."[17] The *there is* can be called a nocturnal space, a space filled with darkness, a space full of the nothingness of everything. Night and darkness can, in a sense, present the *there is* precisely because in the darkness of night there is presence of absence and absence of presence: the presence of darkness is the absence of all beings from one's vision. In the phenomenon of the nocturnal, one can, then, get a glimpse of the *there is*, a glimpse that would anchor the *there is* beyond the merely imaginary and that would, in a certain fashion, fulfill the oppositional expressions with which one speaks of the *there is*.

While the darkness of night has the character of a phenomenon, there is a mythical counterpart to which Levinas could also have referred the *there is*. In the darkness of Hades, there is not even the promise of a coming dawn but only perpetual darkness. In Hades there is, as in night, a presence of absence and an absence of presence. Those who have succumbed to their mortality and no long stride across the surface of the earth or sail the boundless sea are present in Hades. And yet, in their very presence, they are absent, are mere shades. Odysseus cannot succeed in embracing the phantom that is his mother.

Levinas alludes to a further concretization, to a further extension in the direction of content: "Darkness, as the presence of absence, is not a purely present content. It is a matter, not of 'something' that remains, but of the very atmosphere of presence, which, to be sure, can appear later as a content, but which originally is the impersonal, nonsubstantive

---

16. Ibid., 95; *Le Temps et L'autre*, 26.
17. Levinas, *De L'existence à L'existant*, 94.

event of the night and the *there is*."[18] If the darkness of night offers a glimpse of the *there is*, then a certain connection is exposed between the *there is* and such elemental phenomena as night and darkness. Also, as Levinas says, there is a connection between the *il* of the *il y a* and the *il* of *il pleut* and of *il fait chaud*. Is it through an extending of such connections to the elemental that the *there is*, this very atmosphere of presence, can, as Levinas says, "appear later as a content"?

Levinas introduces the elemental in the course of his analysis, in *Totality and Infinity*, of things and of the properly human relation to things. This relation consists in our living from (*vivre de*). The things that we live from, things as we live from them, are not objects of representations, nor are they means of life, nor are they tools or implements in the sense developed by Heidegger in his analysis of the world of everyday Dasein. They are, rather, things to enjoy, and living from them is a matter of enjoyment (*jouissance*). Alimentation figures prominently here: "To live from bread is therefore neither to represent bread to oneself nor to act on it nor to act by means of it." Rather, to live from my bread is a matter of enjoyment: "Enjoyment is the ultimate consciousness of all the contents that fill my life—it embraces them."[19]

On the one hand, then, Levinas extends the sense of things and of our relation to them: he does not limit them to mere objects or to implements but, extending their scope, refers them back to a form of human comportment (namely, enjoyment) that embraces all things, whatever the ways in which they may be further determined. There would seem to be no limit, and the scope of the things from which we live would extend even to the point of bordering on the elemental: "We live from 'good soup,' air, light, spectacles, work, ideas, sleep, etc."[20] Yet, on the other hand, Levinas insists on a strict limitation with respect to the properly human relation to things, a limitation entailed by the primacy accorded to nourishment and alimentation ("all enjoyment is ... alimentation"),[21] a limitation the consequences of which are virtually unlimited. It is a limitation on alterity, a reduction of the alterity of things: Levinas says that the very essence of enjoyment is "the transmutation of the other

18. Ibid., 104.
19. Levinas, *Totalité et Infini*, 83.
20. Ibid., 82.
21. Ibid., 83.

into the same."[22] Thus, the introduction of enjoyment as the properly human relation to things serves, in the end, only to reconstitute, even if at a more concrete and comprehensive level, the determination of the relation that has been taken as governing all modern philosophy and that is indeed displayed in a strain—but only *a* strain—of German Idealism: the determination by which to comport oneself to an object is to appropriate the object, that is, to cancel its otherness and affirm its sameness with oneself. As in eating.[23] As if, contrary to what Heidegger's analysis (the very analysis from which Levinas so insistently differentiates his own) shows, things could not withhold themselves from appropriation. As do, for instance, the sky and the earth. And perhaps even everything elemental in—or at the limit of—nature.

Regarded against the background of this limitation, it is all the more remarkable how Levinas goes on to describe the elemental in ways that would seem to open human comportment beyond the limits of enjoyment as alimentation. Levinas' primary intent is no doubt to show through these descriptions that the properly human relation to the world is, as he says, "irreducible and anterior to the knowledge of that world."[24] The question is whether these descriptions also serve to show that the human relation to the world is irreducible to enjoyment, at least to enjoyment as the transmutation of the other into the same, as the suspension of alterity for the sake of interiority.

Levinas begins his account of the elemental with a reference to enjoyment: the things we enjoy come to us "from a background from which they emerge and to which they return."[25] In other words, it is in a medium (*milieu*) that things take shape and within which we take them up in the enjoyment they offer us. Levinas enumerates some of the forms assumed by these media in which things come to and pass from us: "They are found in space, in the air, on the earth, in the street, along

---

22. Ibid.
23. On the question of eating well as a sheltering of the alterity of things, allowing them to operate as a sign or symbol even of the divine (in its absence), see my paper "Bread and Wine," *Philosophy Today* (1997). See also the interview with Jacques Derrida conducted by Jean-Luc Nancy: "'Il faut bien manger' ou le calcul du sujet," in Jacques Derrida, *Points de Suspension: Entretiens* (Paris: Galilée, 1992).
24. Levinas, *Totalité et Infini*, 103.
25. Ibid.

the road."²⁶ He does not specify just how the things we enjoy emerge from these media, which, as he continues, he will identify as the elemental. How do things emerge, for example, from the air, and how, once we have enjoyed them in some manner or other, do they return to air?

In this opening move two features of Levinas' account become immediately evident, two features that from the outset expose the account to decisive questions. First of all, the sense of the emerging and returning remains indefinite; in particular, these are not regarded at a fundamental level where they would indicate the manner in which things appear as such and withdraw either as such or in their very appearing. To think human comportment to the medium or elemental only in this indefinite, less than fundamental manner is to pass over the place and role of the elemental in the configuration in which things come to show themselves. Thought in this way, the elemental has no bearing on the manifestation. It is as if things came to light and offered us enjoyment without being sustained by the earth and illuminated by the sun, as if they could offer us enjoyment without having already become manifest.

The second feature that comes into question at the outset of Levinas' account concerns his identification of the locus in which things take form and "in which we take hold of them."²⁷ What is decisive in this regard is that the elemental medium is not thought *from nature*. Despite the effort that Levinas makes to differentiate it from a system of operational references like those that Heidegger shows to be borne by a tool, that is, from products of human τέχνη, his enumeration of examples of media includes not only natural loci but also the street and the road. Yet, whatever shows itself appears in space, in the air, on the earth, but not necessarily in the street or along the road. In this regard φύσις has priority over τέχνη. Levinas' second enumeration is still more indicative of the lack of differentiation in his account, of his failure to think the elemental as an element of nature. For the enumeration reads: "earth, sea, light, city."²⁸ Only when finally he focuses on the necessity of differentiating between elementals and things, does his enumeration limit itself to natural elements: wind, earth, sea, sky, air. And then: the sky, the earth, the sea, the wind.

---

26. Ibid., 104.
27. Ibid.
28. Ibid.

Levinas maintains that in contrast to a system or surface of objects linked by operational references, an elemental medium displays a thickness or density (*épaisseur*), which serves to withdraw it from all efforts to possess it in the manner that we possess things. In this connection he concludes: "Every relation or possession is situated within the nonpossessable, which envelopes or contains without being able to be contained or enveloped."[29]

Here again there are two assertions that are open to question. There can be no question but that we are encompassed by the elemental, that, as Levinas expresses it, we are steeped in it, always within it, bathed in it. Yet, this way of being in the elemental cannot be determined as alimentation, not even in its generalized sense. To comport oneself to the elemental—and one will always already have comported oneself to a manifold of elementals—is decidedly not to appropriate it. One cannot cancel its otherness and affirm its sameness with oneself. It withdraws from every effort to appropriate it and displays thereby its alterity. If, furthermore, the elemental is thought at the fundamental level where it is determined as belonging to the structure of manifestation, its alterity proves all the more decisive.

In this connection the second question concerns the sky. In accord to an extent with Levinas' assertion, one can agree that most elementals display a thickness or depth: consider the concealed depth of the earth, which is yet manifest as concealed, or the proverbial thickness of fog. And yet, there is an exception: the sky has neither thickness nor depth. A clear, diurnal sky is sheer recession, pure shining. If one could ascribe depth to it, it would be a depth so peculiar that one would be prompted to say also that it has no depth. The sky is absolute recession, absolved from depth as such.[30]

Levinas points out that an elemental has a certain indeterminacy in that it shows only one side while leaving all others unseen. There is the blue surface of the sea and the cool edge of the wind. Yet, further, an elemental is one-sided in a distinctive manner: the one side shown is not, as with things, a profile within a horizon that harbors innumerable other profiles any one of which could be observed from another perspective. But—in addition to what Levinas mentions—one must also note that

---

29. Ibid.
30. See my account in *Force of Imagination: The Sense of the Elemental* (Bloomington: Indiana University Press, 2000), 181–83.

this feature bestows on each elemental a certain unique concealment, a kind of concealment that occurs as a withdrawal into a hidden depth. While the sea indeed shows itself as surface, that surface appears as a surface to which there belongs a hidden depth; the sea cannot be only surface.

Because we are encompassed by the elemental, we cannot, according to Levinas, either approach it or possess it; the question may be left open whether these terms cohere at all with the other moments of the discourse on the elemental. Yet, despite these impossibilities, Levinas contends that there is a way in which, though encompassed by the elemental, though interior to it, one can nonetheless surmount it. He writes: "Man has overcome [*a vaincu*] the elements only by surmounting this interiority without an exit [*sans issue*] by the domicile, which confers on him an extraterritoriality."[31] And yet, can one simply escape the interiority of immersion in the elemental by taking up residence in a domicile or even, as Levinas mentions, by engaging in activities that refer somehow to the domicile: cultivating the field, fishing in the sea, cutting wood in the forest? Is it not, on the contrary, the case that in taking up residence in a domicile proper, one does not escape the bounds of the elemental, does not become extraterritorial, but rather shelters oneself within the elemental? Fleeing to one's home as a storm approaches does not allow one to escape from the storm but only to shelter oneself from its force. Cultivating the field, fishing in the sea, and cutting wood in the forest do not open a path beyond the field, the sea, or the forest but rather constitute certain kinds of human comportment to these elementals in which one is encompassed.

Levinas draws a rigorous distinction between the elemental and objects, as well as between the elemental and substance. The elemental, he writes, manifests itself as "without origin in a being"; neither is it in any way determined by objects, but rather, it "comes to us from nowhere."[32] And yet, though granting the necessity of this differentiation of elementals from things, this does not require depriving the elemental of all directionality. The approaching storm comes up the valley. Lightning spans the gap between the clouds and the earth. The tide ebbs and flows.

---

31. Levinas, *Totalité et Infini*, 104.
32. Ibid., 105.

Granted the necessary differentiation, there seems nonetheless to be no grounds for concluding, as Levinas does, that the elemental with its proper concealment constitutes "an existence without existents."[33] For it is by no means the case that elementals are devoid of things, of existents. The forest has its trees, the mountain its boulders, the sky its clouds. If nothing stood on the earth, if it supported nothing, it would not be the earth.

Levinas then goes on to add, without further elaboration: "This way of existing without revealing itself, outside of being and the world, must be called mythical. The nocturnal prolongation of the element is the reign of the mythical gods."[34] One could say: the self-withholding of the elemental, its withdrawal either into fathomless depth or into unlimited recession, a withdrawal that is neither simply revelation nor concealment—this is the mythical. It is the scene where the mythical gods reign, that is, where they come to appear in their sovereignty and to remain concealedly aloof in their very appearance.

But the fathomless depth of the elemental is not only to be called mythical. Levinas calls it also "an opaque density without origin, the bad infinite, or the indefinite, the *apeiron*." And in reference to it he writes—quite surprisingly—of the "materiality of the elemental non-I" and of "the fathomless obscurity of matter."[35] That he invokes here the concept of matter marks a serious regression in the analysis—at least in two ways. First, to conflate the elemental with matter in its complete formlessness, its utter indefiniteness, effaces the specificity of the elemental, renders it impossible to distinguish and to delimit even minimally the various elementals. Second, employing the concept of matter in order to characterize the elemental threatens to reinscribe the entire discourse on the elemental within the most classical philosophical conceptuality. Furthermore, it overlooks the most originary possibility: for the introduction of the elemental has the capacity to put thoroughly into question the concept of matter in favor of a more ancient figure that can no longer be termed a concept, a figure that can be renewed as the enchorial space delimited by earth and sky.

Thus, finally, having converged ever more upon it, Levinas links the concealment of the elemental to the *there is*: the nocturnal dimension,

---

33. Ibid., 116.
34. Ibid.
35. Ibid., 132.

he says, is the *there is*. Thus: "The element extends into the *there is* [*L'élément se prolonge dans l'il y a*]."³⁶ Again Levinas refers to enjoyment, but now as encountering a kind of limit in the *there is*, or rather, in the element that Levinas appears in this regard to privilege: "Enjoyment, as interiorization, runs up against the very strangeness of the earth" [à étrangeté même de la terre]."³⁷ No doubt, then, as Levinas says, enjoyment proves to be limited in its freedom; the moment of enjoyment is not insured against what lurks in the very element from which the things of enjoyment come.

The elementals are, then, other than beings, yet without being simply devoid of beings. Within the confluence of elementals that make up a storm, there are things subject to its violence, animals that flee to their shelters, and perhaps humans who retreat to their protective abodes. Yet, elementals must be rigorously distinguished from objects, from things of all kinds. In a way that is more radical than that of beings, elementals are utterly resistant to panoptic vision and to the concepts abstracted from such alleged vision. While encompassing beings, elementals withdraw into a depth or a recession resistant to measure; though we are surrounded by them—occasionally by rain and storm, always by earth and sky—there is no common measure between us and the gigantic elementals.

Their alterity is, then, other than the alterity that lies in "the epiphany of the face."³⁸ It is other than the alterity of death. It is an other alterity, an other otherness, an otherness other than the otherness of other kinds, which are themselves other than one an-other. As the repetition sets in, one realizes that no concept is less controllable, less prone to compound itself, than that which would be said in the word *other*. One may then recall the discourse in Plato's *Sophist* in which it comes to light that, unlike all other kinds, the other is other than itself—which comes down to saying that it neither is a kind nor is divisible into kinds. Even to say that the otherness of the elementals is another kind of alterity is to speak in a way that is not sustainable, that must be cancelled as soon as it is said. If the elementals can be said to display another kind of alterity, then the reference can only be to a kind of kind other than kind.

36. Ibid., 116.
37. Ibid.
38. Ibid., 188.

But, then, the question must be posed: Is enjoyment the only way, the all-encompassing way, of comporting oneself to the elemental? Is it the only way in which, for instance, to comport oneself to the mythical as announced in the elemental, announced not as something apart but as the very withdrawal of the elemental? Could an epiphany of the gods, their appearance on the scene of the mythical, evoke nothing but enjoyment and self-reversion? Or could the elemental—without being reduced to, recast as, the mere *there is*—provoke an ekstasis irrecoverable by enjoyment and its interiorizing movement? Could the elemental provoke a comportment that, rather than leading to self-reversion, would be drawn along in the withdrawal, responsive rather than reactive to the very strangeness of the earth?

7
OBJECTIVITY AND THE REACH OF ENCHORIAL SPACE

All the moves to be traced in the following inscriptions follow a portion of the same trajectory. It runs from the domain of things and their proper objectivity to space as such and beyond to the space bounded by earth and sky and finally to enchorial space, which marks both the *terminus* of the trajectory and the anteriority to which all things are gathered. The first part of the essay follows the course leading from the determination of objectivity to space and its distinctive spacing. The second part, beginning with space as such, concretizes it as the expanse stretching from earth to sky, which, broaching the determination—or nondeterminability—of enchorial space leads finally to absolute anteriority.

1.

Objectivity will never be dispelled. It cannot be made to vanish leaving no trace. It cannot be rendered null and void. Never can it simply come to nothing. Regardless of how we name them, whether we call them merely *things* or by another of the many names accorded them, regardless also of what concepts—or nonconcepts—we bring to bear on them, regardless of how we set about to understand what precisely they are, they are there. In everyday factical life, for one who is entirely caught up in providing life's necessities, but also in theoretical, scientific endeavors, for the most remote observer whose telescope intercepts the light of a star that is distant, both in space and time, by millions of light-years—in these and in all other connections, things are there. In their being there, they have (in distinction, perhaps most notably, from what is merely phantasized) what can—though of course need not—be called objectivity.

Even in Nietzsche's radical inversion of Platonism, even in this move by which his thought advances to the limit of metaphysics, things—or what are called things—perdure. Even when, in bringing the inversion to its culmination, Nietzsche writes, emphatically, that *"with the true world we have also abolished the apparent world!,"*[1] this can only mean that the apparent character of the world has been abolished, that the things of this world are no longer to be regarded as remote appearances of the allegedly true world. Yet in whatever way they are regarded, as appearance or otherwise, these things perdure; they remain *there*, they simply—or perhaps not so simply—are there.

In the statement that things are there, two basic assertions are entailed. The first is that they are there *for us* if we turn our attention to them. In other words, our senses are attuned to them in such a way that, whenever we are in some way there with them, they can come to be apprehended through vision, audition, or other senses. The second assertion is that they are there *in and of themselves*, that their being there does not depend on their being apprehended. They are there regardless of whether their sensible presence is matched by an apprehension by one whose senses are attuned to such presence. This character of being in and of themselves is what has been called the *objectivity* of things. Regarded in this manner, things have, in modern philosophy, come to be called *objects*. The word has its appropriateness, as do, in German, the near cognate *Objekt* and the near synonym *Gegenstand*. What these words say quite directly is that things stand over against us, that they are cast up before us. In short, they are there in and of themselves.

Thus it can be said that we—by *we* I mean, collectively, the being that each of us *is*—that we sustain a double relation to things. On the one hand, because they are there in and of themselves, we are separated from them; or, perhaps more precisely, they are detached from us and remain so even as we attentively approach them. The relation is, then, one of separation or detachment. On the other hand, things are accessible to us; they can be approached in such a way as to be disclosed in their sensible presence, can be brought to show themselves to our

---

1. Friedrich Nietzsche, *Götzen-Dämmerung*, vol. VI/3 of *Werke: Kritische Gesamtausgabe* (Berlin: Walter DeGruyter, 1969), 75.

sensible apprehension. Hence we sustain with them a possible connection, an adherence in which we are exposed to their sensible presence, a sense-enriching propinquity or proximity to things. Günter Figal formulates this double relation quite precisely. He writes: "It belongs to appearing essentially that it occurs at a distance. . . . The separation here is at the same time a connection; something is away from me, therein 'withdrawn' [*darin 'entzogen'*], only therefore there for me."[2]

This double relation in its full complexity was also a theme in the early development of German Idealism, most conspicuously in Reinhold's *Elementarphilosophie*. In his work *The Foundation of Philosophical Knowledge* (1794), Reinhold maintained that the *Elementarphilosophie* must begin with a single, foundational, self-evident first principle—a *Grundsatz*. This principle takes the form of a description of a self-revealing fact of consciousness; it puts aside all metaphysical presuppositions regarding the nature of the subject and of the object, even those that Kant assumed such as the dualism of sensibility and understanding. The principle itself is stated thus: "In consciousness representation is distinguished through the subject from both object and subject." In another, more direct formulation, the principle reads: "Representation is distinguished in consciousness by the subject from the subject and object and is referred to both."[3] The principle is thus expanded into a fourfold configuration: (1) The subject refers representations to itself, since there must be a subject who has the representation and is aware of having it. In other words, a representation must be *for someone*. (2) The subject refers its representation to the object, since it must be a representation of something. (3) the subject distinguishes the representation from the object, since the representation cannot be identical with what it represents. (4) The subject distinguishes the representation from itself, since the one who represents is not the same as the representation itself. Therefore, by orienting his account to the representation, Reinhold charts the complex in which the subject, relating to itself, distances itself from the object, and, on the other hand, connects itself both to itself and to the object. If, in reference to this complex, one abstracts from the subject's relation to itself, then it is reduced to the twofold described in Figal's

---

2. Günter Figal, *Gegenständlichkeit: Das Hermeneutische und die Philosophie* (Tübingen: Mohr Siebeck, 2006), 151.
3. K. L. Reinhold, *Über das Fundament des philosophischen Wissens* (Jena, 1794), 78. The second formulation comes from *Beiträge zur Berichtigung bisheriger Missverständnisse der Philosophen* (Jena, 1790).

succinct statement: in its relation to the subject, the object displays both separation and connection.

The question that emerges marks the center of a basic—if not *the* basic—philosophical configuration. It is the question of how this double relation can be sustained, of how these almost contradictory moments of detachment and adherence, of separation and proximity, can be operative at the same time, in the same regard, and between precisely these terms. How can we be both separated from things, while yet coming into proximity to them? How can things be there in and of themselves, and yet, from precisely there where they are, show themselves as being there?

Hegel formulates this question as a matter of the identity of opposites. In his early work, especially in *Belief and Knowledge*, he finds the key to its solution in the Kantian categories, in Kant's conception of the categories as determinations both of thought and of appearances—that is, in Hegel's idiom, as, at once, determinations both of the object and of the subject. According to Hegel's interpretation, what makes possible this identity of experience and its objects, of thought and intuition, of subject and object, is the transcendental imagination. Yet Kant grasps this identity only within the narrow scope of the categories, leaving all other moments, the allegedly a posteriori moments, completely outside it. Hegel's move is to extend the identity without limit. Here is the account he gives in a very remarkable passage in *Belief and Knowledge*:

> The imagination [is] not to be understood as the middle term that gets inserted between an existing absolute subject and an absolute existing world, but rather as what is primary and originary and as that out of which the subjective I and the objective world first separate themselves, as the sole in-itself [*Ansich*]. This imagination is the originary two-sided identity, which, on the one side, becomes subject in general and, on the other, object, and originarily is both and is nothing other than reason itself.[4]

Thus, for Hegel, subject and object, we and things, are both separated and connected by the force of imagination. Insofar as imagination is conceived as an originary identity from which separation proceeds, Hegel's account accords a certain priority to the unity or connection of subject and object, anticipating the identity of thought and being from

---

4. G. W. F. Hegel, *Glauben und Wissen*, in vol. 4 of *Janaer Kritische Schriften, Gesammelte Werke* (Hamburg: Felix Meiner, 1968), 329.

which and to which the *Science of Logic* proceeds. Yet insofar as the originary identity is already two-sided even prior to the separation of subject and object, the priority is moderated and perhaps retracted entirely.

In this regard there is a certain affinity between Hegel and Heidegger. For Heidegger, too, in his interpretation of Kant, takes the imagination to be originary, to be, in Kant's own phrase, the common root of thought and intuition. Hence, it is that by which concurrent separation and connection between subject and object—that is, *a priori* synthetic knowledge—is possible.

Heidegger's appropriation of the *Critique of Pure Reason* in his book *Kant and the Problem of Metaphysics* remains still controversial, though there can be no doubt as to its radicality. In this appropriation—to put it in global terms—the Kantian task of laying the foundation of metaphysics mutates into the pursuit of the question of the sense of Being; and the transcendental imagination, regarded as the pure self-affective forming of time expressed in the schemata, mutates into Dasein. To be sure, Heidegger raises the question also of space, the question—prompted by the second edition of the *Critique of Pure Reason*—as to whether space as well as time belongs to the transcendental schematism. Yet, rather than pursuing this conjunction, Heidegger takes this ambivalence as an indication that time cannot be grasped in its fundamental character as long as it is conceived as a pure succession of nows. In the end, Heidegger is explicit: "The originary ground that is revealed in the laying of the foundation is time." With the appropriation thus prepared, Heidegger writes: "The laying of the foundation of metaphysics arises on the basis of time. The question of Being, the fundamental question of a laying of the foundation of metaphysics, is the problem of 'Being and Time.'"[5] This expression refers of course to the Sache, but also the punctuation indicates explicitly that it refers primarily to the work *Being and Time*.

It is remarkable that, after his book on Kant, Heidegger largely abandons the problematic of imagination, despite the enormous role it played in the appropriation of Kantian critique to fundamental ontology. In *The Origin of the Work of Art*, he declares—without further ado—that it is questionable whether the essence of poetry, the work of

---

5. Martin Heidegger, *Kant und das Problem der Metaphysik*, vol. 3 of *Gesamtausgabe* (Frankfurt a.M.: Vittorio Klostermann, 1991), 202f.; hereafter cited as *GA*, followed by volume and page number.

art in general, and the happening of truth can be sufficiently thought on the basis of imagination. As if to emphasize its dismissal and seal its fate, Heidegger uses conjunctively both words for imagination: *Imagination* and *Einbildungskraft*.[6] This is the last mention of imagination in the artwork essay, indeed the only mention in the entire essay.

In later writings there are a few isolated passages in which Heidegger's discourse on imagination is briefly resumed. In *Contributions to Philosophy* there is a passage—a single, short, isolated section—in which Heidegger situates Dasein within the domain of the imaginal, using the term *Einbildung* rather than *Einbildungskraft*, presumably in order to stress, as he says, that this discourse has to do neither with transcendental imagination nor with imagination as a power of the soul. He links it rather to *Ereignis* and characterizes it "as the happening of clearing [*als Geschehnis der Lichtung*]."[7] What is perhaps most notable about this passage is that there is no development as regards the operation and role of imagination, nothing comparable, for instance, to the analysis of the schemata in the *Kant and the Problem of Metaphysics*. Rather, imagination is now completely detached from its Kantian context and simply, almost as if in passing, inserted—without further consequence—into the elaborate configuration that is unfolded in *Contributions*. Much the same can be said of the very brief reference to *Ein-bildung* (now hyphenated) in the essay "Poetically Man Dwells," except that in this case it is into a primarily Hölderlinian context that imagination is inserted. As generated from the term *Bild*, which, for Heidegger, denotes that which lets the alien be seen in the look of the familiar,[8] the word itself, now hyphenated, disempowered, and pluralized, is thoroughly alienated from what, since the ancients, has been called imagination.

Despite the extended analysis of imagination that forms the heart of Heidegger's Kant-interpretation, discourse on the imagination is entirely lacking in *Being and Time*. Indeed in the existential analysis, Heidegger sets out on a very different course by which to take up the question of objectivity. As if taking it into account that things are there in and of themselves and yet show themselves to us from precisely there where they are, Heidegger focuses, not on the synthetic power of imagination, but rather, indeed exclusively, on the *there* (the *Da*). His task

6. See Martin Heidegger, *Der Ursprung des Kunstwerkes*, in *Holzwege*, GA 5: 60.
7. Martin Heidegger, *Beiträge zur Philosophie*, GA 65: 312 (§192).
8. See Martin Heidegger, *Vorträge und Aufsätze*, GA 7: 204f.

becomes that of analyzing the *there*, of distinguishing its moments, and of demonstrating phenomenologically how these moments are gathered into the operation of the *there* by virtue of which we sustain a double relation to things, that is, both separation and proximity. In other words, it is a matter of showing how we *are there* in proximity to things—hence the designation *Dasein*—and how, on the other hand, things are there in and of themselves, that is, objectively. What is of utmost significance is that on both sides the effect of the analysis is deconstructive. Thought from—in reference to—the *there*, the subject is deconstructed and mutates into Dasein. Likewise, determining the sense of objectivity from—in reference to—the *there* has the effect of deconstructing objectivity, so that what emerges as objectivity, as the basic character of things as there in and of themselves, radically displaces the classical determination, for instance, as being-in-itself. The first and, in *Being and Time*, most thoroughly developed stage of this deconstruction takes place in the reversal of *Vorhandenheit* into *Zuhandenheit*.

What supports and ultimately makes possible these moves is Heidegger's development of the concept—if it can still be called a concept—of world. The *there* is reconstrued as world; the subject's being-there, its Dasein, is redetermined as Being-in-the-world; and the mode of being of objects is reconfigured as their innerworldly being, their character as *innerweltlich*. Because of the way in which they are there within-the-world, they are separated from us, are there in and of themselves; they are objective in this deconstructive sense. Because of the way in which we are there in-the-world, in the very world within which things come to pass, we enjoy the proximity to them that allows them to show themselves to us from *there* where they—and where we too, though differently—are.

Despite all the differences—consciousness now displaced by Dasein, *Vorhandenheit* made derivative from *Zuhandenheit*, subject and object reconstrued as being-in-the-world and innerworldly being—there is in this account a certain affinity to Reinhold's analysis. For Heidegger it is from world that what previously figured as subject and object have their distinctive relation; for Reinhold it was representation that provided such mediation.

Since the entire existential analysis and the fundamental shifts that it would effect hinge on the concept of world, there is little wonder that Heidegger's analyses of it are so intricate and, in a sense, extend throughout the two published Divisions of *Being and Time*. Many of these analyses, for example, that of *Zuhandenheit*, have been interpreted again and again in various connections, interpretation layered upon interpretation in a complex pattern of congruence and incongruence. It is not my aim here to peel away these layers nor to gauge their various incongruities. Rather, in order to raise the questions that are my concern, I will take up only two specific developments.

The first of these developments proceeds from a distinction between two forms of the *there*, between two ways in which the *there* occurs. On the one hand, it retains the sense of world such that in being there we can encounter beings as they show themselves from there where they themselves are. On the other hand, the *there* has the sense of space, that is, of the disseverant (*ent-fernend*), directional spatiality of Dasein and of the regional orientation and multiplicity of places belonging to innerworldly beings. There is a certain structural correspondence or duplication between these two senses. This is indicated by Heidegger's conjunction of the following two statements: first, "Dasein is essentially disseverant [de-distancing—*ent-fernend*]"; and, second, "it lets any being be encountered in its proximity as the being that it is."[9] Heidegger's analysis of spatiality unfolds almost entirely from this determination, which, in turn, mirrors—though in its specificity—that of the *there* in the sense of world.

One of Figal's major contributions consists in his marking the insufficiency of Heidegger's analysis. In his words, the analysis "does not make sufficiently clear the status of what is spatially discovered and discoverable, and, due to this, the character of space itself also remains underdetermined."[10] Figal's analysis of Dasein's character as de-distancing, as bringing into proximity, is carried out in a much more intensive and concrete manner. As throughout much of *Objectivity*, he draws very productively and insightfully on Husserl's work and thus develops his analysis in a way that is more explicitly phenomenological. By means of this analysis, Figal succeeds not only in providing a more differentiated and structurally precise account of spatiality but also in showing how the determination of space points beyond to the questions of freedom, language, and time.

According to Heidegger's more general analysis, the spatiality of innerworldly beings is determined by the totality of references within which these beings are what they are. The implication is, then, that their

---

9. Martin Heidegger, *Sein und Zeit* (Tübingen: Max Niemeyer, 1969), 105.
10. Figal, *Gegenständlichkeit*, 160.

spatiality is grounded on world, just as Dasein's directional proximity to things is grounded on its character as Being-there in-the-world. The consequence is decisive: along with the structural correspondence between the two senses of *there* (as world and as spatiality), there is also a grounding relation, namely, of spatiality on world.

The second of the two developments that I want to take up comes in the midst of Division 2. It occurs at that stage of the analysis where, having uncovered the ecstatical character of temporality, Heidegger turns back to the existentials described in Division 1 and reinterprets them within the context of temporality. Let me excerpt and string together a brief series of passages from the relevant analysis. Heidegger writes, emphasizing the sentence by setting it entirely in italics: "*The existential-temporal condition of the possibility of world lies in the fact that temporality, as an ecstatical unity, has something like a horizon.*"[11] He continues: "There belongs to each ecstasis a 'whereto' of raptness [*ein 'Wohin' der Entrückung*]. This 'whereto' of the ecstasis we call the 'horizonal schema.'" One could pause at this point to consider how in the expression "horizontal schema" Heidegger is retrieving the Kantian schematism that figured so prominently in his interpretation of Kant. But instead, let me press forward, noting that Heidegger proceeds to characterize the schemata of each of the three ecstasies and then concludes: "On the basis of the horizontal constitution of the ecstatical unity of temporality, something like a disclosed world belongs to the being that is always its *there*." Heidegger declares even that the transcendence of the world, its reaching out beyond all innerworldly beings, is grounded on the ecstatical character of temporality, on its reaching out to future and pastness. The consequence is, again, decisive: world is grounded on temporality. But then, so too is spatiality, as Heidegger explicitly declares in the culminating section (§70): "Hence Dasein's specific spatiality must be grounded on temporality."[12]

The result of the two developments could not be more decisive: spatiality is grounded on world, which, in turn, is grounded on temporality.

Thirty-five years later, in the lecture that reverses the title of *Being and Time*—as the never-published Division 3 was to have done—it is quite otherwise. In "Time and Being," he writes: "The attempt in *Being and Time* §70 to derive the spatiality of Dasein from temporality is

---

11. Heidegger, *Sein und Zeit*, 365.
12. Ibid., 366.

untenable."[13] Now, in the lecture, he speaks of time-space (*Zeit-Raum*—hyphenated) and connects it to the happening of clearing (*Lichtung*).

In fact, this move from the grounding relations elaborated in *Being and Time* to the reformulation in terms of *time-space*—or, more properly, the mutation of the earlier configuration into that of *time-space*—was already effected in the late 1930s, most notably in *Contributions to Philosophy*. Here, too, *time-space* is linked to the clearing, which in turn is expressed as the essence of truth: "Time-space is merely the essential unfolding of the essence of truth [*die Wesensentfaltung der Wesung der Wahrheit*]."[14]

Let me conclude by sketching another alternative. This other alternative renews certain moments in Heidegger's analysis and yet advances in a decisively different direction. This development not only grants, with Figal, the limits of Heidegger's analysis but also is intended to strike a certain resonance with Figal's eminently concrete analyses and with the expansion of the problematic of space that he achieves thereby.

If Heidegger's analysis is construed topographically, then there will be two points from which, along parallel but distinct lines, Heidegger advances to his account of world and hence to a deconstructed sense of objectivity. These two points, which stabilize and determine the entire analysis, represent, respectively, imagination and the there. But—to broach the alternative—let us suppose that instead of being traced as two distinct lines, they were allowed to intersect, to cross and intertwine, perhaps even to coalesce into an entirely different figure.

With the first point, imagination, a shift would be required at the outset in order to situate the analysis outside the scope of the Kantian schematism and its elaboration in *Kant and the Problem of Metaphysics*. It is a shift that, though in a different context, occurs already in German Idealism, most notably in Fichte and the early Schelling. In the very briefest formulation, it is a shift from the conception of imagination as a power of synthesis to that of imagination as a hovering (*Schweben*) between different terms in such a way as to hold them together in their difference. The latter conception can be illustrated by the example of phantasy: to imagine a phantasy scene requires not only that it be present before the mind's eye, that is, intuited, but also, since it is not itself

---

13. Martin Heidegger, "Zeit und Sein," in *Zur Sache des Denkens*, GA 14: 29.
14. Heidegger, *Beiträge zur Philosophie*, GA 65: 368 (§242).

given through sense, that it be brought forth, produced. Thus, in such an act of imagining, imagination comes to hold together the moments of intuition and production, yoking them together in their very difference. Such a conception could also be brought bear on our comportment to elemental nature, on the way in which, for instance, earth and sky are gathered so as to bound the enchorial space in which things come to pass.

In connection with this operation, a space must be opened and sustained, a space within which, across which, different moments can be drawn together in their difference. It is this space that can be identified as—or as a mutation of—the *there* of Heidegger's analysis. For, from the outset of that analysis, the *there* is precisely the locus where separation and proximity are operative together in their difference. There it is—in the space of imagination—that things can show themselves as sensibly present and yet also be in and of themselves. There it is—in the space of imagination—that objectivity in its full sense comes to pass.

In the opening of such space, it is not a matter so much of ground (*Grund*) as rather of abyss (*Abgrund*)—that is, such opening has an abyssal character. For it is not as though a certain space is already there, though somehow closed off, enclosed by boundaries. It is not as though boundaries simply need to be effaced, not as though the space needed only to be opened up into a broader space to which it would then belong. Rather, it is a matter of the space that any such space already presupposes, of the very *there* where any opening, any effacing of boundaries, would take place. Yet, though presupposed, it cannot simply have been there as objects are there, for it is itself the very *there* where, were this the case, it would itself have to have been. It is thus a space that must be opened, and yet it is nothing apart from the opening. In short, it is a *spacing*.

The task would be, then, to show that and how the spacing of imagination unfolds into a spacing of the world. In other words, what is needed is a rigorous analysis capable of demonstrating how the hovering of imagination in which abyssal spacing occurs, lets something like a world with its various kinds of horizons take place. A way would, then, have been traced from the spacing of imagination to the possibility and structure of objectivity.

This trace would in effect reinscribe Fichte's celebrated declaration that all reality is brought forth solely by imagination. For then—now, or rather, in the time to come, in the coming time-space—it could be declared that all things show themselves to us from there where they are—that, in other words, there is objectivity—because it is there that imagination takes flight.

2.

Space is unapparent. It does not appear as do things in space. Yet it is not simply concealed, not entirely sealed off beyond the reach of experience. Though space does not appear, it is somehow there along with all the things that do appear. As Figal expresses it: while space itself never appears, "it is, in its own way, 'there,' together with that which appears."[15] Yet even in this seemingly straightforward determination, there is enacted a circularity, a turning back on itself, which attests to the complexity and self-referentiality of such a venture: in saying that space is *there*, that it is *together* with apparent things, one presupposes spatial determinations in the very determination of space. To be sure, there is a way of breaking out of the circle, namely, by distinguishing between the space to be determined and another space, a protospace, a space before space, which would provide a basis for the determination. Space could, then, be declared to be there in this space before space. And yet, what could such a protospace be—assuming that it is, or else exemplifies, a *what* and indeed assuming that it *is* at all, in a determinate sense of being.

As unapparent, space is not a phenomenon in the ordinary sense of something that directly shows itself. Yet, since, while being itself unapparent, it is together with the things that appear in it, it can be termed a phenomenon in the phenomenological sense defined by Heidegger at the outset of *Being and Time*. Heidegger begins with the formal concept of phenomenon and the corresponding concept of phenomenology as letting be seen that which shows itself from itself. He then sets out to deformalize these formal concepts so as to arrive at the phenomenological concept of phenomenon. It is a question of what phenomenology is to let be seen. Heidegger's answer: "Manifestly it is something that does not show itself initially and for the most part, something that is *concealed* in contrast to what initially and for the most part does show itself. But, at the same time, it is something that essentially belongs to what initially and for the most part shows itself, indeed in such a way that it constitutes

---

15. See Günter Figal, *Unscheinbarkeit: Der Raum der Phänomenologie* (Tübingen: Mohr Siebeck, 2015), 17.

its meaning and ground."[16] In other words, a phenomenon in the phenomenological sense is something unapparent that somehow belongs in a fundamental way together with that which appears. As letting the unapparent be seen, phenomenology is thus preeminently suited to take up the task of bringing space to show itself. Indeed Heidegger offers as examples of such phenomena the Kantian forms of intuition, that is, space and time.[17]

Yet, space is not only the space of things. Discourse, too, has its space. One speaks somewhere, and one's voice resonates in tones determined by the surrounding space. The sound may be echoed, and its import may be subtly shifted by one's spatial situatedness. Furthermore, one casts one's voice across the space between oneself and those to whom one speaks. Written discourse, too, has its space, its spacings, which sets its elements apart while also conjoining them across the space separating them. Even the slightest variation in this spacing, a misplaced comma, for instance, can alter significantly what is said and what is meant thereby. There is a close parallel with the appearing of things: as things appear, so discourse signifies; and just as the space in which things appear is itself unapparent, so the spacing of discourse does not itself signify. Nothing is said by the space between two words or by the comma separating them. And yet, while saying nothing, the spacing of discourse must be operative in order that something be said. Insofar as hermeneutics, in the more classical sense, concerns the interpretation of texts, of discourse as such, and an analysis of the conditions underlying interpretation, it will be paired with phenomenology in the task of making manifest this unapparent spacing.

The specific theme to which we now turn concerns what might very tentatively be called another kind of space. In this connection the word *kind* will have to be displaced somewhat from its usual sense. Both Kant in the *Critique of Pure Reason* and Figal in his recent book *The Unapparent*[18] recognize that space cannot be regarded simply as a generic kind

---

16. Martin Heidegger, *Sein und Zeit*, 35.

17. Ibid., 31f. This connection provides one way—though there is also another—in which to understand the subtitle of Figal's book *The Unapparent: The Space of Phenomenology* (*Unscheinbarkeit: Der Raum der Phänomenologie*).

18. "Space is not a discursive or, as one says, general concept of relations of things in general, but a pure intuition" (I. Kant, *Kritik der reinen Vernunft* [Hamburg: Felix Meiner, 1956], A24f./B39). Figal characterizes space in general as a *Leerstelle* (*Unscheinbarkeit*, 28f.).

under which would be ranged various specific kinds. It is rather, as must be said of the χώρα, a matter of a kind of kind beyond kind.

This other kind of space that is not properly a kind is the space delimited by earth and sky. Its impropriety is reflected in the fact that it is a kind of which there is only one instance. This space is unapparent; for the most part our sense apprehension is directed to the things encompassed by this space. Indeed, virtually all the things and events that matter to humans take place in this space—all the things that are rooted in the earth or that bestride its surface; all the elements that come upon us from above, light, rain, snow; and all that has its abode somewhere between the upper and the lower bounds, wind, clouds, and, in a different way, the soaring peaks of mountains.

And yet, while the expanse delimited by these bounds is indeed unapparent, it is by no means simply concealed. It lies openly before us; or rather, it encompasses us to such an extent that, even when it becomes the focus of attention, it cannot be brought to stand over against us as though it were an object. Unlike space in general, the expanse between earth and sky is not a space between two things. For it has been recognized, at least since the time of Galileo, that the sky is not, even in a superior sense, a thing, that it is not, as Ptolemaic astronomy supposed, a heavenly sphere in which the stars are fixed. There is no such thing as the sky; and while it persists as bounding the space in which things and elements come to pass, it is also the opening onto the cosmos, not as a limit that, while fixed, would be surpassed, but rather as itself dissolving in that very opening.

Neither can the other bound of this space be regarded as a thing from which the space would expand toward the sky. In this regard one can appropriately refer to the late manuscript by Husserl that undertakes to show that the earth is not a mere place for things but rather is the ground (*Boden*) on which things can have a place and on which human endeavors can be carried out. There is a series of expressions by which Husserl characterizes the earth: *der Stammboden, die Urheimat, die Urheimstätte, die Arche der Welt*. The last of these expressions has a double sense: it refers both to the Greek ἀρχή (origin, basis) and to an ark, which, as in the biblical story, would be supportive of the lives of earthly creatures.[19]

---

19. The manuscript by Husserl is *Grundlegende Untersuchungen zum phänomenologischen Ursprung der Räumlichkeit der Natur*, in *Philosophical Essays in Memory of*

This space of earth and sky encompasses us, as it does virtually all things that matter to us, all the things and persons that we cherish or fear, all that we advance toward or flee from. Even things that we merely imagine or that we remember show themselves as situated within this space. In imagining something, we not only bring it to show itself as if it were perceived but also transpose ourselves imaginatively into the position of the one who perceives it. For instance, in imagining a certain kind of landscape, one imaginatively situates oneself at a certain place from which the landscape is viewed. In this way one also sets oneself within the space of earth and sky in which we already would, independently of the imaginative act, have been situated. Rather than providing an escape from our situatedness in this space, such acts of imagination double our placement within this space.

In our way of being always already cast into this space bounded by earth and sky, we are not related in the same way to these two bounds. To one of these, the earth, we are by nature bound. Even when the age-old dream of flight is realized, the earth remains the basis, the ark, from which and back to which flight is undertaken. Only when the opening of sky onto the cosmos occurs does the possibility arise of altering the bond to the earth; but then, with the dissolution of the upper bound, the space itself is displaced.

As earthbound, humans by nature cast their vision beyond toward the sky, both aspiring to the heights and yet wary of the danger that ascent—in its various metaphoric transpositions—poses. This natural comportment with its opposite directionalities is presented artistically in Paul Klee's lithograph *Tightrope Walker* (*Seiltänzer*). The figure is poised on the high wire far above the ground, having ascended the ladder depicted toward the edge of the work. Yet, as earthbound, he is threatened by the constant danger of falling, against which he defends himself by his very upright posture (emphasized by the vertical column that passes through his chest and head) and by the long pole with which he maintains his balance.

Thus, as encompassed by the space of earth and sky, we earthbound humans also cast our vision across the expanse of this space. Yet, granted this natural comportment, there are other modes of comportment that

---

Edmund Husserl, ed. M. Farber (Cambridge, MA, 1940), 307–25. See my discussion of this manuscript in "The Question of Origin," in *Double Truth* (Albany: State University of New York Press, 1995), chap. 3; also in Figal, *Unscheinbarkeit*, 242.

not only extend across this expanse but also reflect back upon us, drawing us into a certain disposition. In certain exceptional cases, philosophy has undertaken to trace such modes of comportment.

At the outset of his book *Nature*, Emerson writes of solitude and of the way by which one can retire into solitude.[20] He begins with the observation that to go into solitude requires not only retiring from society but also from engagement with language, in which others would remain tacitly present: "I am not solitary," he says, "whilst I read and write, though nobody is with me." By what means, then, can one retire into solitude? Granted the exclusions of society and of language, what mode of comportment has the capacity to draw one back to oneself? Emerson answers: "But if a man would be alone, let him look at the stars." Though he knew very well what modern scientific cosmology had discovered regarding the nature of the stars, Emerson's reference here is to the stars as they are viewed by unaided vision in the nocturnal sky—that is, as they mark the upper bound of the space of earth and sky. He alludes even to this space, construing it in the guise of the atmosphere, and to its expanse as expressed in the sublimity of the stars. He writes: "One might think the atmosphere was made transparent with this design, to give man, in the heavenly bodies, the perpetual presence of the sublime." He observes that if the stars should appear only one night in a thousand years, man would adore the sight and would preserve the memory of it for many generations. But the wonder is that they are to be seen on almost any night.

Yet, granted the wonder of the stars, how is it that their sight provokes the retreat into solitude? What is it about the stars that draws us back into ourselves? Emerson's answer could not be more direct: "The stars awaken a certain reverence, because though always present, they are inaccessible." Thus, for Emerson, the withdrawal into solitude, the turn back to oneself away from the self-dispersion through society and language, the turn through which one is given back to oneself, is not simply the result of activating an inner reflexivity. It is not merely a matter of turning one's vision away from everything else and casting it into one's own interiority—to echo Fichte's prime imperative. For Emerson, on the contrary, it is through a certain kind of turn outward, through

---

20. Ralph Waldo Emerson, *Nature*, in *Selected Writings of Ralph Waldo Emerson*, ed. Brooks Atkinson (New York: Random House, 1940), 3–42. *Nature* was first published in 1836.

OBJECTIVITY AND THE REACH OF ENCHORIAL SPACE 115

a casting of one's vision toward the inaccessible beyond, that the turn inward is accomplished. It is from the upper bound of the space of earth and sky that one is driven back into oneself. It is not, then, by turning one's vision away from everything else that one is enabled to withdraw into oneself but, rather, precisely by stretching one's vision across the vast expanse. It is not even that, having thus extended one's vision, one would then withdraw it in the movement of return to oneself. Rather, it is precisely as extending to the stars that vision is sustained in its turn inward. In solitude one would be also there alone with the stars.

The ancients, too, looked to the stars, and ancient philosophers traced the course on which vision extended to the stars and returned to oneself. A celebrated passage in Plato's *Timaeus* became the paradigm for most later undertakings of this sort. Near the end of the first of Timaeus' three discourses, the discussion focuses on vision and, in particular, on the benefit that vision provides for mortals and for which the gods bestowed it upon them. Timaeus declares that vision is indeed what brings about the greatest benefit, since, as he says, "none of the accounts we are now giving about the all [περὶ τοῦ παντός] would ever have been uttered if we had seen neither the stars nor the sun nor the sky [οὐρανός]."[21] In other words, the very possibility of philosophy depends on the vision of the sky and of the movements traced there by the stars and the sun.

Timaeus proceeds to indicate more specifically how it is that vision provides the greatest benefit. It is a matter of uranic vision and of the mimesis that becomes possible through it. In the most decisive passage, Timaeus declares that the god bestowed vision upon us "in order that, by observing the circuits of νοῦς in the sky we might use them for the revolvings of thinking [διανόησις] within us, which are akin to those, the disturbed to the undisturbed; and by having thoroughly learned them and partaken of the natural correctness in their calculations, thus imitating the completely unwandering circuits of the god, we might stabilize the wandering revolvings in ourselves."[22]

The course that Timaeus traces is not entirely unlike that traced by Emerson. In both cases there is operative a vision of the sky, either of the stars set against it or of the movements, the circuits, to be seen there. The difference in the visions lies in the character that, in each case

---

21. Plato, *Timaeus*, 47a.
22. Ibid., 47b–c.

respectively, these markings in the sky are taken to have. In the case of Emerson, what is decisive is the remoteness of that toward which vision is cast, the fact that the stars are present yet inaccessible. In the Platonic instance, vision occupies itself with the orderly, noetic character of the movements of the sun in the diurnal sky and of the stars in the nocturnal sky. In regard to this case, it is imperative to recognize that neither the possibility nor the consequence of such vision is undermined by the knowledge that we have—as did Emerson also—that, considered in terms of modern, scientific cosmology, the movements in the sky are not perfectly orderly, that they are not even orderly in the complex way proposed by Ptolemaic astronomy. Today, for instance, it has been observed that the rotation of galaxies does not follow the regular course that, on the basis of the gravitational forces of the visible bodies in the galaxy, it should follow; accounting for such rotation thus requires—or at least is currently taken to require—that something unseen, so-called dark matter, be posited. Yet, whatever the character of the movements may have proven to be, it remains the case that to natural, unaided vision, the sky appears as a place where the stars move in orderly revolutions. It is of such vision and only of such vision that Timaeus speaks. It is worth noting, however, that in the classical period the Greeks were quite aware that there were movements in the nocturnal sky that were not so orderly, namely, the retrograde movement exhibited by the planets. Even in Timaeus' declaration about the noetic, undisturbed circuits that vision beholds in the sky, there is a subtle reference to such errant disorder, namely, in the use of words based on πλανάω, to wander about, words thus akin to πλάνης, planet.

Yet, the casting of vision toward the markings and movements to be seen in the sky constitutes only one moment in the relatedness that eventuates. Along with it there is also the reflection back from what is seen; something pertaining to the visionary self is reflected back to it in such a way as to engage the self. For Emerson this engagement occurs as a return to oneself from the self-dispersion otherwise wrought by society and language. The vision of the stars issues in a withdrawal into oneself, a gathering of oneself to oneself, that is, a retreat into solitude. In this connection the affinity of Emerson's thought to that of German Idealism becomes evident. In both cases there is a casting of the self outside itself, into or onto something exterior to it; and then, in turn, there is a return of the self to itself. Within the context of German Idealism the question is whether, through the return to self, the exteriority to which it had been cast is dissolved as such, that is, *aufgehoben*; or whether in some manner it is left intact. In the case of Emerson there is, in this respect, no question but that the inaccessible beyond, the stars, remains untouched by dialectic.

In the Platonic instance, the reflection back from the sight of the sky and of the movements beheld there engages the self in a quite different way. The engagement is not that of returning to oneself so as to gain a certain self-possession, so as to withdraw from dispersion back into self-presence. Rather, through observation and even calculation trained on the orderly revolvings in the sky, one gains the capacity to imitate in oneself these undisturbed, unwandering circuits. It is not a matter of gathering the self into itself but rather of a celestial mimesis by which order and stability would be installed in oneself.

In the *Timaeus,* this song of celestial mimesis is heard just as Timaeus' first discourse is approaching its end or, rather, just before Timaeus interrupts it and declares that they must launch a new beginning. This interruption is occasioned by a certain interruption in the fabric of the first discourse, that is, by a certain dissonance that is sounded just as Timaeus is about to commence his song of celestial mimesis, just as he sets out to celebrate the great circle linking the order of the movements above to the ordering of the human soul. The dissonance has to do with fire, air, water, and earth—to adopt, though with reservations, the conventional translations of πῦρ, ἀήρ, ὕδωρ, and γῆ. The tear that rends the fabric of the first discourse is produced by the failure to account for these, by their having been taken for granted in the account of how the god fashioned the cosmos. It is for this reason that the discourse must be interrupted and a new beginning—a second discourse—must be launched, a beginning that returns to a point anterior to the first beginning, to a point where the formation of fire and the others can be described.

The second discourse cannot, however, begin with fire and the others, for there is—in a sense of *is* that becomes ever more problematic—something else—something that is by no means a thing—anterior to fire, air, water, and earth. It is anterior to these even at the point where they are not yet formed, not yet given the form that the god will later impose on them, that is, even at the point where they are not yet quite themselves. Of this anteriority, which could be called the absolute beginning,

Timaeus gives several designations leading finally to what would be its proper name if it could indeed have a proper name. The name is Χώρα.²³

There is an ancient tradition, going back to Chalcidius' Latin translation of the *Timaeus*, in which χώρα is translated as *locus*, as *place* or *space*. Yet Timaeus' identification of it with the necessity (ἀνάγκη) over which the artisan god has no control, the necessity that rips apart the fabric of the first discourse, points to its uniqueness over against space in the usual sense. It is indeed unapparent in a radical sense, for, as Timaeus declares, it cannot be grasped by ordinary sense perception. Rather, it appears only on the occasion of being watery or fiery, and then it appears *as* water or *as* fire. In Timaeus' words: "that part of it that is made fiery appears as fire."²⁴ Hence, though the χώρα indeed appears, it never appears simply as itself. As concealing itself precisely in appearing as fire, it is, in a radical sense, unapparent. As, in the beginning, fire and the others are taken up into the χώρα, they have no form whatsoever; they are amorphous; they are mere traces of themselves.

Timaeus' account goes on to indicate that the χώρα is indeed still more withdrawn—that is, even more radically unapparent—than its nonperceptibility entails. It is withdrawn from vision in that the condition in which it appears—in and as fire, for instance—will always already (in particular, for us) have been surpassed through the god's imposition of form. In this respect, the χώρα and the traces it receives are anterior to the cosmos, indeed anterior to the space of the cosmos as it will be formed by the god; the χώρα would be a protospace, a space before space. Of such a space we could at most only somehow catch a glimpse behind what the god would already have fabricated; or, as Timaeus finally declares, we might come upon it in a dream and have it then in view in what, upon our awakening, might remain from the dream. The χώρα also cannot be apprehended in the guise of the sheer emptiness (*die Leere*) of space in general; only much later in the *Timaeus* and on the basis provided by the chorology, does Timaeus take up the theme of the void (τὸ κενόν).²⁵

---

23. The following discussion of the χώρα draws on my much more extended and detailed account in *Chorology: On Beginning in Plato's "Timaeus"* (Bloomington: Indiana University Press, 1999), chaps. 3 and 4.
24. Plato, *Timaeus*, 51b.
25. Ibid., 58b. Figal develops an extended discussion of the χώρα, though he stops short of offering a detailed commentary on the passages in the *Timaeus* that would seem most pertinent to this theme. He takes up, though in his own way, the tradition

The χώρα also withdraws from λόγος and from the images that can be called up by means of λόγος. To be sure, Timaeus offers a number of images of the χώρα; but what is most remarkable is that they are conflicting images that cannot be gathered into a single coherent depiction; they clash and undermine each other. Perhaps most conspicuously, the images of the χώρα as nurse, as the "in which" and "from which" of generation, and even as receptacle cannot be reconciled with the images of it as gold that can be molded into all possible figures and shapes and as a mass of wax on which a seal can be imprinted. Little wonder, then, that Timaeus says of the χώρα that it is "most difficult to catch."[26]

That none of these images quite succeeds in catching the χώρα is a consequence of its very nature as the third kind (τρίτον γένος). As such, it is to be distinguished from the εἴδη that constitute the first kind and from the images of these εἴδη that constitute the second kind. Thus, it cannot properly be called by any name signifying an εἶδος (as all but singularly proper names do); neither can it be properly represented by any image, as if it were of the second kind. It is because of this radical withdrawing that Timaeus confesses that the χώρα can be touched only by a sort of bastard discourse.

How, then, is the affinity between the χώρα and space to be thought? There is a passage in Book 3 of the *Republic* that suggests a peculiar affinity between the χώρα and the lower bound of the space of earth and sky. What specifically is said in this regard is set within the context of a fabricated story that displaces into a dream that which the citizens of the πόλις have actually undergone. Enacting the role of one who would tell the noble lie, Socrates says that he will attempt to persuade the citizens "that the rearing and education we gave them were like dreams; they only supposed they were undergoing all that was happening to them, while, in truth, at that time they were under the earth within, being fashioned and reared themselves." He continues the story: "When the job had been completely finished, then the earth, which is their mother, sent them up. And now, as though the χώρα they are in were a mother and nurse, they must plan for and defend it, if anyone attacks, and they

---

stemming from Chalcidius' Latin translation. Distinguishing χώρα from various specific senses of space, Figal appears to identify it—though without saying so explicitly—with space in general or space as such (*Raum* überhaupt). He notes also that as concealing itself precisely in appearing as fire, it is, in a profound sense, unapparent (Figal, *Unscheinbarkeit: Der Raum der Phänomenologie*, 38–56).

26. Plato, *Timaeus*, 51b.

must think of the other citizens as brothers and born of the earth."[27] So, the citizens are to be told that they were formed, shaped, educated within the earth and were born from the earth. They are told this story primarily as a means of forging their bond to the χώρα they now occupy. Yet, the χώρα now occupied, the territory in which the πόλις is located, is not interior to the earth but rather extends across its surface. The bond that the story fabricates connects the embryonic condition within the earth to the defense of the πόλις: because the citizens were formed and nurtured within the earth and born from mother earth, they can now be enjoined to defend the territory that the πόλις occupies on the terrestrial surface. And yet, on the earth the citizens live and move, not merely like shadows on the surface, but rather standing upright and casting their vision upward across the celestial expanse. While their χώρα is bound to the earth, it has as its full expanse the space of earth and sky, which may, accordingly, be termed enchorial space.

By forging a connection between the χώρα and enchorial space, one circumvents the consequence that is risked if, instead, the χώρα is too closely allied with space in general. For the latter can all too readily dissolve into the isotropic space of early modern philosophy. In turn, then, the χώρα can be assimilated to Cartesian *extensio* or at least regarded as anticipating the modern conception. Such a reduction will long since have lost sight of that bastard discourse in which, in the *Timaeus*, the χώρα is suspended.[28]

But how, then, is the connection between the χώρα and the space of earth and sky to be thought in a way that avoids such reductionism and yet, without abandoning the Timaean chorology, takes this connection up into the venture of thinking the space of earth and sky as the unapparent place of all that is elemental? Certainly the connection cannot be one of simple identity; in any case, to think it in this manner would not prove productive for such a project. On the other hand, it could perhaps be advanced by taking the χώρα as a kind of schema from and through which to rethink the nature of enchorial space (which is, in turn, the space of nature). Then, for instance, the discourse on the χώρα as receptacle might provide a means for rethinking the way in which both the elements and the things they encompass are set within the compass of

---

27. Plato, *Republic*, 414d-e.
28. So far as can be determined from the few brief remarks by Heidegger regarding the χώρα, his interpretation tends in the direction of such a reduction. See Martin Heidegger, *Einführung in die Metaphysik*, GA 40: 71.

the most comprehensive elements, earth and sky. In addition, Timaeus' declaration that the χώρα is invisible, that it never shows itself as such but only in and through the elemental showings that occur within it, may provide a means for rethinking the unapparentness of enchorial space. It is, then, by way of such an elemental schematism that a phenomenology of enchorial space can be ventured. Such phenomenology would require a vision receptive not only to what can be rendered manifest but equally to what in its very appearance withdraws leaving only a trace of its retreat from our vision.

8 THE SCOPE OF VISIBILITY

Although there are many ways in which the visibility of things is limited, there are also multiple paths along which vision can exceed these limits. The visionary course on which humans find their way is compounded from these limits and the lines—or circles or spirals—along which the limits are exceeded and visibility extended.

Every particular field of vision is bounded by a horizon of things that, though unseen, are implicated by what is directly displayed to vision. Vision has only to follow the lead of these implications in order to shift the horizon and render visible the things previously unseen. Visibility is thus extended to these things through an exchange in which, simultaneously, it is withdrawn from other things.

Even the visibility of things actually seen has its limits, for at any moment these things reveal themselves only as they appear to a particular perspective: the sides that are turned away remain hidden, and those that are turned obliquely show themselves in distorted shapes that are not true to the things themselves. Yet, just as the field of vision can be extended or changed entirely, any particular perspective can be exchanged for another. Sides previously unseen or seen only distortedly can thus be brought to appear as they truly are, but only through an exchange in which the previously frontal sides are displaced and the limit is reconfigured.

Things display other aspects that lie beyond the limit of visibility in ways that do not allow such direct exchanges to take place. For instance, in order to render visible the interior of a densely solid object, it may be necessary to shatter the object and thus to destroy it as such. Among those aspects that lie beyond the limit of visibility in such a way as to preclude exchange, most prominent are those that are directly displayed only to senses other than vision. The warmth of a sunbaked boulder, will never be seen, even though the sight of the intense illumination on its surface will come, by way of synesthetic implication, to supplement the touch to which alone the stone's warmth is directly revealed. The fruitiness of a fine Riesling is not to be apprehended visually, even though the wine's appearance in the glass (its color, its viscosity, etc.) communicates across the senses with its taste. The aroma of freshly baked bread may arouse one's appetite and prompt a search for its source, but the sight of even the most perfectly formed loaf will never reveal the aroma. Listening to the second movement of Beethoven's Sixth Symphony may well evoke an imaginative vision of a pastoral scene, and this vision may indeed supplement the music and lend a certain fulfillment to the experience. Reading the printed score of the symphony may also, for the musically trained eye, promote a more astute listening. But listening is imperative if the sublime tones that constitute the music itself are to be revealed.

All such aspects, reserved for senses other than vision, lie beyond the limit of vision; there is no means by which they can be brought within its scope and rendered visible as such. And yet, vision extends toward them by bringing a certain visible aspect to bear on them. Through its synesthetic blendings vision supplements the disclosures afforded by the other senses; on what they directly disclose, it bestows a certain disjunctive visibility. Its bearing may be compounded insofar as the rich metaphorics of vision comes into play to compensate for the paucity of descriptive language geared to the other senses. In these connections vision both endures its limits and yet also exceeds them, extending the scope of visibility.

Thus, within visual comportment as such there are operative movements by which variously posed limits are exceeded while also in a certain respect remaining intact and providing the measure of this very excess. Through such movement the visibility of things is, in various dimensions, extended beyond what is simply and actually displayed before vision.

A new stage in this extension of visibility is inaugurated in the birth of modern science. When Galileo turned the newly invented telescope to the heaven, the sight he beheld revealed that the limit of visibility to natural vision was much narrower than had hitherto been supposed; the narrowness of the limit was revealed precisely through the exceeding of this limit that became possible by means of the telescope. Through his discovery that the number of stars is more than ten times greater than could be seen by unaided vision, Galileo both marked the limit of visibility to such vision—marked it precisely as a limit—and extended the visibility of the heaven on beyond the limit. The sphere of the so-called fixed stars, previously taken as the outer boundary of all that is, thus came to be dismantled; the indefinite space that proved to extend on beyond opened the possibility of hitherto inconceivable extensions of vision to astral phenomena that lay ever farther beyond the limit of what is visible to natural vision. The progressive enhancement of instrumentation, leading eventually to such things as fields of radio telescopes and telescopes that, like the Hubble, are no longer earthbound, has made it possible to carry out such extensions of vision, such expansions of visibility, to an extent so enormous that it becomes ever more difficult to envisage what is revealed.

For Galileo, as for the ancients, it was self-evident that the cosmos beyond is revealed to vision and to vision alone. Though fancies were indeed entertained about a music of the heavenly spheres, the hearing of such music could never quite be detached from the visual observation of the orderly movement of the stars; neither could it quite be identified with the audition of actual sounds. With the Galilean dismantling of the Ptolemaic spheres, these fancies were put to rest once and for all. Even today it remains self-evident that, in principle, the cosmos is revealed only to vision, since the modern enhancements of astronomical instrumentation serve either to provide more distinct visual images of distant phenomena or to extend reception to a range of the electromagnetic spectrum much broader than that of light. Vision of the heaven has never ceased to be celebrated for its power to open the human spirit beyond itself and beyond the confines of the earthly environment to which, until very recently, humans have been bound. One can hardly imagine what the result would have been, had humans been denied vision of the stars; they would most certainly have found their way in the world quite differently and would have been bound to orientations quite other than those that actually came to govern human comportment.

Among the ancient celebrations of the power of vision, there is one that has remained both paradigmatic and a continual source of wonder. It is found in Plato's *Timaeus*, at a crucial juncture in the dialogue where the discourse on the formation of the cosmos is about to be interrupted for the sake of an entirely new beginning. The passage is one in which the discourse turns upon itself so as to account for the possibility of the very account of the cosmos that has just been given by Timaeus. Having spoken of the power of the eyes, Timaeus continues: "Now according to my account, vision [the power of sight—ὄψις] has come to be the cause of the greatest benefit for us, since none of the accounts we are now giving about the all [περὶ τοῦ παντός] would ever have been proclaimed if we had seen neither the stars nor the sun nor the heaven [οὐρανός]." He goes on to explain that the vision of the heaven and of the alternations and circulations that it brings has taught us about number and about time and has made possible our inquiry into the nature of the all. Thus it has given us philosophy, than which there is no greater, god-given gift. He concludes: "Now this, I say, is the greatest good of eyes."[1]

Yet now there is still more cause to celebrate, now that vision can be extended to what seem the farthest reaches of the cosmos. Through what they have revealed, these extensions of visibility have aided in the formation of more comprehensive concepts of space and time and of the basic formations and processes operative in the cosmos. They have both prompted and made it possible to confirm theoretical formulations that would otherwise not have been ventured or that, at best, would have remained thoroughly problematic. Hence, the modern extension of visibility has served to enhance the gifts of vision to an extent hitherto hardly conceivable. Yet it bears also on what the Platonic text designates as the greatest of these gifts, not, however, by supplying results that would constitute philosophy anew but, rather, by offering provocations that require of philosophy that it return to its own beginning.

In its beginning philosophy measures and extends the range of visibility. At least in the beginning inscribed in the Platonic dialogues—which is already another beginning, a new beginning, a second sailing—the visibility of natural things is marked by way of differentiation from other visibilities. The extension thus traced beyond the visibility that natural things display to unaided vision reaches, however, into an entirely different order. The visibility that this extension opens upon is

---

1. *Timaeus*, 47a–b. For more extended accounts of the three passages discussed here, see my books *Chorology: On Beginning in Plato's "Timaeus"* (Bloomington: Indiana University Press, 1999) and *The Figure of Nature: On Greek Origins* (Bloomington: Indiana University Press, 2016).

fundamentally other than both those operative in natural vision and those effected by instrumentation—indeed so fundamentally other that it comes to define the very sense of fundament. It is a visibility in the emergence of which the natural visibility of things tends in a sense to be effaced. In this respect it is not unlike the visibility of a phantasy image that one brings before one's inner, imaginative vision and with which one can become so enthralled as to become oblivious to the surrounding natural appearances.

That the fundament or origin or cause of things—of their being as they are—has the character of an emergent visibility is marked by the designations εἶδος and ἰδέα. Both words are derived from the verb εἴδω (obsolete in the present active, replaced by ὁράω), which means to see, to behold, to look: an εἶδος or ἰδέα is simply the look that something presents when one looks at it. It is that which, under certain conditions, for a certain kind of looking, comes to appear to vision, gains a certain visibility.

In the philosophical extension of visibility, three stages can be identified and outlined by reference to particular passages in three Platonic dialogues. In extracting these passages from their dialogical context, the utmost precaution is required; for each dialogue is a unique blend of discursive, mythical, and dramatic elements that inform every segment of the dialogue. Thus, it is only with extreme reservations that one can justify separating particular passages from the context woven by these elements. In orienting consideration of a particular passage to a specific theme such as visibility, one cannot but interrupt the bearing that by virtue of its context the passage has on a host of other thematic and dramatic concerns.

The first of the three passages occurs near the center of Book 7 of the *Republic*. This Book begins with the story of the cave, of the prisoner's escape from its obscurity and of his ascent into the light above. In a sense the story of the cave not only opens Book 7 but also constitutes it as a whole. For what follows the opening narration of the story and runs on to the end of the Book is a series of seven repetitions of the story in various guises.[2] The passage to be considered occurs in the fourth repetition and hence, structurally, at the center. Preceded by a segment in which Socrates and Glaucon discuss the necessity of κατάβασις—that

---

2. See my discussion in *The Verge of Philosophy* (Chicago, 2008), pp. 38–40.

the philosopher must go back down into the cave—the central repetition of the story tells of the ἀνάβασις, of the means, the disciplines, by which the philosopher-to-be would be led upward from attachment to visible things toward the vision of what truly is.

The first such discipline is described initially as "learning about the one [περὶ τὸ ἕν μάθησις]"; such learning is then identified as calculation (λογιστική) and arithmetic (ἀριθμητική). It is significant that from the outset this learning is linked to vision: Socrates declares that this discipline is among those most apt to lead "toward a looking at that which is [or: toward the vision of being—ἐπὶ τὴν τοῦ ὄντος θέαν]."[3]

The passage proper extends this discussion. Socrates says that such learning "leads the soul powerfully upward and compels it to discuss numbers themselves." He continues: "It will not at all permit anyone to put forth in discussion numbers that are attached to visible or tangible bodies."[4] Socrates explains the necessity of such detachment by referring to the requirement rigorously adhered to in Greek mathematics: that the *one* be regarded strictly as *one*. More specifically, since all numbers are composed of *one*s, each number being precisely a number *of ones*, no one can be considered different from any other *one*; and being strictly *one*, it cannot be cut so as to become two or broken up so as to become many. Thus, Socrates states the axiom of those who know of such things: "each *one* equal to every other *one*, without the slightest difference between them, and containing no parts within itself."[5] This requirement is what guarantees the distinctive determinacy of numbers and of counting.

It is because of this requirement that the arithmetician will not admit numbers that are attached to visible or tangible bodies; no such body is capable of being a *one* in the sense that arithmetic requires, but rather in every case such bodies are different from one another and are subject to being cut in two or broken into a multitude of parts. Yet, if numbers are not attached to visible things, then they are not to be apprehended in the same manner as such things; they will have no share in the visibility of such things and will not be grasped by means of sense (αἴσθησις). Indeed this is the conclusion Socrates draws: these numbers (the *one*s recognized by those who know of such matters) "admit only of

---

3. Plato, *Republic*, 525a.
4. Ibid., 525d.
5. Ibid., 526a.

being thought [διανοηθῆναι] and can be grasped in no other way."⁶ And yet, what is decisive is that in escaping sense in the direction of thought, numbers are not entirely deprived of visibility. Socrates puts forth an imperative for those who are genuinely to learn about numbers: they are "to engage in" this learning "until they come to a vision of the nature of numbers [ἐπὶ θέαν τῆς τῶν ἀριθμῶν φύσεως] with thought itself [τῇ νοήσει αὐτῇ]."⁷ To grasp numbers by way of thought is to come to have a vision of them; it is to apprehend them in their distinctive visibility, in the visibility that is extended to them precisely as they are detached from things visible simply through sense. Their visibility is a dianoetic visibility compounded with invisibility to sense, their apprehension a seeing compounded with not seeing.

Much the same can be said of the subsequent discipline that Socrates introduces, geometry, and indeed, in varying connections, of all such disciplines. Geometry does not have to do with what "comes to be and passes away,"⁸ nor with deeds (such as squaring and adding) applied to such things. Rather, in Socrates' words, geometry "compels one to look [θεάσασθαι] at being."⁹ The triangle that is the subject of geometry is not the figure drawn in the sand but, rather, a figure detached from sense, one that, invisible to sense, is to be apprehended only through dianoetic vision. Such visibility is of another order than that of sense; it is a visibility extended beyond sense and compounded with invisibility to sense.

The second of the three passages also addresses such an extension beyond the visibility of sense, yet it does so in a way that moves beyond mathematics toward the more strictly philosophical. It is found in the *Theaetetus*, at the very end of the long first part of the dialogue devoted to Theaetetus' thesis that knowledge (ἐπιστήμη) is perception (αἴσθησις). Just prior to the passage Socrates has stressed the ascensional orientation of the philosopher, illustrating it by way of the story of Thales, the oft-cited story of how he was so preoccupied with studying the heaven above that he fell into a well and became an object of jest for a servant girl. Socrates then consolidates the protracted critique that has preceded by now focusing on the alleged view of the Heracliteans that all is motion,

6. Ibid.
7. Ibid., 525c.
8. Ibid., 527b.
9. Ibid., 526e.

THE SCOPE OF VISIBILITY   129

that there is only the flow of what passes before sense. The import of what he says is that to speak is to determine something as something, to fix it, hence to halt the flow; thus the thesis that all is motion has the effect of rendering λόγος impossible. As Socrates puts it ironically: "But those who speak this speech must set down another voice, since now at least they do not have the words for their own hypothesis."[10] Their view, dissolving all determinacy into the flow, reduces them to silence.

As the passage proper opens, Socrates has just compared their situation to that of people who, in a gymnasium, play at a tug-of-war in which they stand in the middle between two opposing teams, represented by the Heracliteans and the Eleatics. They are pulled, in turn, in both directions, now toward those who set everything flowing, now toward those who arrest all things. It is between these, between limitless flow and static determinacy, that the conversation in the passage is stretched.

In the passage, Socrates examines the comportment by means of which we come to apprehend things. His intent is to distinguish a moment that, while exceeding mere perception, is essential to the apprehension—indeed to the knowledge—of things. The result is, on the one hand, that Theaetetus' thesis identifying knowledge and perception is definitively refuted; but, on the other hand, it is shown precisely what must be brought to supplement perception so as to yield knowledge.

In a sense the result is already implied by the very first step. Setting aside Theaetetus' initial supposition that it is by our eyes that we see white and black things (and correspondingly for hearing), Socrates induces his interlocutor to acknowledge the basic distinction that the entire remainder of the passage will only elaborate: the eyes are that through which we see (δι' οὗ ὁρῶμεν), not that by which we see (ᾧ ὁρῶμεν). In other words, the eyes and the other senses are merely instruments (ὄργανα) by which various perceptions come to us. But the mere presence of manifold perceptions gained through the senses does not suffice for us to see or hear something. Socrates explains: "For it's surely strange [or: dreadful, marvelous—δεινόν], my boy, if many perceptions sit in us as if in wooden horses, but all these do not stretch together [συντείνει] into some one look [ἰδέα], whether soul or whatever it must be called, by which we perceive through these, as if with

10. Plato, *Theaetetus*, 183b.

instruments, all perceptible things."[11] The initial distinction between that through which and that by which we see is thus elaborated on the side of that which is yielded by each. Through the senses, various perceptions (αἰσθήσεις) come to be present in us, like Achaian soldiers in a wooden horse waiting to be drawn through the gate of Troy. Yet these perceptions alone do not suffice for the perception of perceptible things; rather, they must stretch together toward and into a look that is otherwise apart from them. It is only by way of this look toward which the perceptions stretch together that we—that is, the soul or whatever it must be called—come to perceive perceptible things. Thus—almost paradoxically—perceptions alone do not yield perception; rather, perception occurs only in and as the stretching together of perceptions into one look. Perception of things occurs only in the advance from what is seen through the eyes to a look that belongs to another order of visibility. Perception of visible things requires that there be operative an extension of visibility beyond that of perceptions.

Socrates proceeds to determine the character of the look, contrasting it with the perceptions that stretch toward it. Ascertaining that what is perceived through one sense-instrument (through one power [δύναμις], as he now terms it) cannot be perceived through a different power, he turns first of all to a question concerning numbers, to a question of ones and of two. Referring to sound and color, he declares that both are two and that each of the two is one. His question to Theaetetus concerns the numbers that different perceptions (through different powers) can have in common, as well as other determinations such as the same and the other, being and not-being, any of which can be had in common by different perceptions. Specifically, the question concerns that through which such commons are apprehended, granted that they cannot be apprehended through any power of sense. He asks: "So through what do you think [διανοεῖ] all this about them? For it is possible neither through hearing nor through sight to grasp what is common to them [τὸ κοινὸν λαμβάνειν περὶ αὐτῶν]."[12] Theaetetus answers that there is no instrument of the sort they have discussed that would be capable of grasping the commons—"but," he concludes, "the soul itself

11. Ibid., 184d.
12. Ibid., 185b.

through itself, it appears to me, looks upon [ἐπισκοπεῖν] what is common to them all."[13]

The look toward and into which the manifold perceptions stretch together thus has the character of the common (τὸ κοινόν); and, to take—as Socrates does—the cases most remote from the perceptions, it may assume the form of number, of same and other, of being and not-being. Asked specifically about being, Theaetetus places it among those kinds "which the soul by itself stretches itself toward."[14] His answer serves to establish a primary connection: the manifold perceptions stretch together toward the common look because the soul by itself stretches itself toward the look, drawing the perceptions along—as if they were Achaian soldiers in a wooden horse being drawn through the gate of Troy. In stretching itself toward the look and drawing the perceptions into it, the soul comes to look upon the common look, and it is through all that belongs with this dianoetic vision that perception of visible things is achieved. It is through a visibility extended beyond what is visible to the eyes that apprehension of visible things in their visibility is made possible.

The third of the passages also addresses such extended visibility, yet it does so in such a way that, rather than turning back to visible things so as to demonstrate how such visibility bears on their perception, it turns toward their origin and the distinctive, indeed blinding, visibility of the origin.

The passage is found in what forms the thematic and dramatic center of the *Phaedo*. This center is framed—and thus marked as such—by two brief reversions to the conversation between Phaedo and Echecrates, the conversation that frames the entire account that Phaedo gives of the words and deeds of Socrates' last day. Since the conversation and the account within it occur in the remote city of Phlius some time after Socrates' death, the reversions serve as a reminder of the distance of Phaedo's account from the event itself. The form thus mirrors the content of the central discourse, which concerns precisely the taking of distance that is effected by having recourse to λόγος.

The central discourse, set off by the framing reversions, culminates in an account to which Socrates gives the form of autobiography.

---

13. Ibid., 185d–e.
14. Ibid., 186a.

Referring to the situation in which, plagued by doubts and objections regarding the deathlessness of the souls, Socrates finds himself in the most dire straits, Phaedo reports that he "paused for a long time and looked to himself."[15] Looking back into his past, into his own philosophical genesis, Socrates proceeds to tell how he became who he is. He tells of the inquiry into nature (περὶ φύσεως ἱστορία) that he ventured by seeking to explain certain natural things by identifying other natural things as their cause (αἴτιον). He tells of how these inquiries were plagued by aporias, especially by those having to do with ones, with their resistance to all explanations geared to natural—that is, visible—things. He tells also of the disappointment he suffered in engaging Anaxagoras' thesis regarding νοῦς.

The passage proper is set against this background. It begins with Socrates asking Cebes: "Do you want me to make a display [ἐπίδειξις], Cebes, of the way by which I have busied myself with a second sailing [δεύτερος πλοῦς] in search of the cause?"[16] Like sailors who, in the absence of wind, take to the oars, Socrates abandoned the sort of inquiries he had pursued and ventured a second sailing.

The passage as a whole is devoted to describing how Socrates came to venture the second sailing and to identifying the distinctive turn by which it is launched:

> Well then after these, since I had renounced this looking into beings, it seemed to me I had to be on my guard so as not to suffer the very thing those people do who behold and look at the sun during an eclipse. For surely some of them have their eyes destroyed unless they look at the sun's image [εἰκών] in water or in some other such thing. I thought this sort of thing over and feared my soul would be blinded if I looked at things [τὰ πράγματα] with my eyes and attempted to grasp them by each of the senses [αἴσθησις]. So it seemed to me that I should have recourse to λόγοι and look in them for the truth of beings [σκοπεῖν τῶν ὄντων τὴν ἀλήθειαν].[17]

The passage begins elliptically. Yet the first words, "After these [μετὰ ταῦτα]," clearly refer to Socrates' previous inquiries, especially to those that attempted to account for natural things by finding their cause

---

15. Plato, *Phaedo*, 95e.
16. Ibid., 99d.
17. Ibid., 99d–e.

in other such things, accounting—to cite Socrates' example—for the stability of the earth by supposing it to be propped up on a pedestal of air. Such inquiries had led Socrates into aporias that made him doubt even what he previously thought he knew. Thus he gave up on these failed inquiries, as he goes on to say: "since I had renounced this looking into beings, I had"—then, subsequently—"to be on my guard" against a certain danger. The danger was, then, one that became threatening only after Socrates had given up looking into beings in the manner of inquiry into nature. It was not a danger incurred by looking into things in this manner but a danger that threatened only after he had renounced such inquiry and moved on toward something else. But toward what did he move on? Instead of looking for the cause among things, he would have sought it beyond things; his search would have been directed toward a cause that would also be an origin (ἀρχή) and that, from beyond things, would let things come forth in the double sense of being illuminated and being generated. Yet that which, from beyond all things, is primarily responsible for their emergence both into the light and as such is the sun. Thus it is that the passage begins by referring to those who look at the sun and to the need to be on guard against the danger of blindness that accompanies such looking.

And yet, strictly speaking, one cannot really look at the sun—not, that is, if looking requires more than an instantaneous glance. To be sure, one can see things in the sunlight, and in a certain way one can even see the light itself as it comes to illuminate things. But one cannot, for more than a moment, look directly at the sun. One cannot look into the very origin of light—*except* during an eclipse. Only then can one gaze directly at it—but then only by exposing oneself to the danger of blinding oneself, of having one's eyes destroyed. Yet even then, since in an eclipse the sun is covered over, one would not really have beheld it; or, at most, one would have beheld it only as it was withheld from vision. In this case the one blinded would not even have gained, in return, a vision of the source of visibility.

In the figure of looking at the sun, an ἀναλογία is implicitly operative. For it is a matter not only of things being illuminated but also of their being visible as what they are, that is, of their showing themselves in and through their proper look. Beyond the common looks would lie the self-concealing origin of the determinate visibility of all things.

The visibility of the origin thus belongs to still another order than that either of visible things or of the common looks that, distinct from sense, render the vision of visible things possible. The origin would enable all other visibilities, and yet its visibility would be precisely such as to be always withdrawn, would be of such intensity that it would always be eclipsed for human vision.

Once he has spoken of the danger incurred by attempting to look into the very origin of things, Socrates addresses again the danger that accompanies the effort to grasp things solely by means of sense: "I thought this sort of thing over and feared my soul would be blinded if I looked at things with my eyes and attempted to grasp them by each of the senses." In this case the blindness Socrates fears is of the sort that previously interrupted his inquiries into nature and left him no longer knowing what beforehand he had thought he knew. The threat of blindness is double: it is incurred both in looking to things and in looking away from things to their origin.

Thus, the Socratic turn, the second sailing, proves to be more complex than might have been supposed. It is a turn that renounces direct vision of natural things but that, at the same time forgoes looking directly into the origin of these things. Thus turning neither to things nor to their origin, Socrates turns instead to λόγοι. The course that he takes resembles that taken by those who protect their eyes by looking "at the sun's image in water or in some other such thing." In Socrates' words: "So it seemed to me that I should have recourse to λόγοι and look in them for the truth of beings."

The second sailing culminates in recourse to λόγοι. The word καταφεύγω also means to flee for refuge, in this case refuge from the double threat of blindness. Yet, taking refuge in λόγοι is to serve as a means of looking for the truth of beings, as a means that escapes the threat. The search for the truth of beings has as its aim to disclose things as what they truly are, and this means to reveal the common look proper to such beings. Yet the look is nothing other than what the *Phaedo* designates as *being* (τὸ ὄν) in the most proper sense, that is, as the selfsame being that in each case determines things so that they are called by the same name as the one determining them.

From what Socrates says, it might be supposed that the λόγοι to which recourse is to be had are images of the beings themselves, that they are like the images of the sun that can be seen in water. However, Socrates immediately denies any such supposition: "Now perhaps in a certain way it is not quite like what I am likening it to. For I do not at all concede that someone who looks at beings in λόγοι looks at them in images any more than someone who looks at them in deeds."[18] Hence, the λόγοι are not merely images of beings that one would behold in the absence of the beings themselves. Rather, the λόγοι serve to open up a way of access to beings, a way appropriate to human knowing, a raft of human λόγοι, as Simmias earlier called it.[19] Socrates' comparison suggests that λόγοι let beings become manifest in in a way similar to that in which a deed makes manifest something about the character of the person who performs the deed.

Yet how do λόγοι allow beings to be made manifest? How does it happen that holding back from the look into the origin and having recourse instead to λόγοι the second sailing advances toward the manifestness of beings? Socrates is explicit about how, in particular, the second sailing commences: "In any case, this is how I begin: on each occasion I put down as hypothesis whatever λόγος I judge to be the most vigorous."[20] In other words, he sets out by taking up a certain comportment to λόγος, a new, additional comportment and a new beginning, since humans always already exist within a comportment to λόγος. This comportment consists in hypothesizing in the precise sense of the word ὑπόθεσις, that is, laying down or setting out a λόγος so as to place it under something. In this setting out of a certain λόγος, Socrates sets out explicitly that which is said in the λόγος, what is intended in and through the words that are spoken. More specifically, he sets out the one beings that are always already meant when one says, for instance, *beautiful* or *good* or *large*. As he explains, he sets out the "beautiful itself by itself and the good and the large and all the others."[21] He sets out the beings themselves *as they are said*, as they are always already operative and manifest in speech. Indeed Socrates identifies what is set out as "the very thing I have never stopped talking about."[22] Ostensibly he is referring to the earlier conversations in the *Phaedo*, which return repeatedly to discussion of the one beings. Yet, these are *always* the very things one will have been talking about; they are what talk is about as such.

18. Ibid., 99e–100a.
19. See ibid., 85c–d.
20. Ibid., 100a.
21. Ibid., 100b.
22. Ibid.

It is only at this point that Socrates introduces the word εἶδος, referring it specifically to the look of the cause (τῆς αἰτίας τὸ εἶδος). Thus he establishes the connection: the one beings that are operative in λόγος and that can be set out from λόγος in a certain manifestness are nothing other than the looks, the common looks, that are the true causes of things. And yet, this connection remains enigmatic: for the one beings are said and are set out as said, whereas the common looks are manifest in their distinctive visibility. There is perhaps no saying just how the visibility of the looks comes—or can come—into an accord with the one beings that are said.[23]

There are, then, two distinct lines along which visibility is extended beyond that of things visible to ordinary vision. The first might be pictured as horizontal; it runs from the exchanges of horizons and of perspectives that are operative in natural vision to the vast extensions made possible by modern astronomical instrumentation. The other line, distinctively philosophical and more vertical, runs from the visibility of natural things to the common looks, which through their distinctive visibility render things truly visible; the line extends on toward the origin but in such a way that it also turns back and, by way of λόγος, renders the looks manifest, manifest as said if less definitely as visible.

The question is whether these two lines, seemingly diverging from a single origin, also curve in such a way as to intersect at some distant point; or whether, at least, they attain sufficient proximity to allow some mutual effect. The question is most pressing in view of the very remarkable phenomena that the instrumentation of modern astronomy has made it possible to discover. For among these phenomena there are some, such as black holes and dark matter, that seemingly are incapable of any visibility whatsoever. While there are necessarily certain effects that allow such phenomena to be detected—those around the event horizon of black holes and those having to do with the gravitation operative in the movement of galaxies—these phenomena are by nature—if in this connection the very concept of nature can remain intact—absolutely resistant to visibility. No enhancement of instrumentation can render them visible, and any visibility projected upon them as one seeks

---

23. For a more detailed account of this portion of the *Phaedo*, see *The Figure of Nature: On Greek Origins*, 227–41.

somehow to envisage them will prove entirely inappropriate, completely unfounded.[24] Such phenomena, violating the very sense of phenomenon, have—and can have—no look whatsoever. Even more insistently than the blinding origin, they withdraw from every look.

With the acknowledgment that there are beings that lie absolutely beyond the limits of visibility, that there are beings to which no extension of visibility can reach, that there are beings utterly beyond the utmost scope of visibility, another beginning would seem to be imperative, one in which being would at such extremes be detached from visibility and from presence to vision. It is perhaps only in this respect that we can at present discern the shape that this beginning must take.

---

24. See my discussion in *The Return of Nature: On the Beyond of Sense* (Bloomington: Indiana University Press, 2016), chap. 6.

9 COSMIC TIME

For the ancients the rising and setting of the sun, marking the alternation of day and night, evoked such wonder as that with which philosophy begins. As they lingered before these wondrous sights, they envisaged, in turn, a step back through which, without dispelling their wonder in the least, they would come to ask about all that is displayed in such sights. What was manifest was the order in the movement of the heavenly bodies: that of the revolution of the heaven and of the rising and setting of the sun, as well as its ascent and decline with the passing of the seasons. In order to determine these orders more closely, measure was put into play in the form of mathematical calculation. It was then only one step—though a very long one—to the beginning of philosophy with its directedness to the ἀρχή or φύσις of all that had been displayed in these wondrous sights. Even once this step had been taken, wonder endured: for wonder not only is the beginning of philosophy but also is what, most powerfully, impels it onward.

Even once philosophy is on its way and has invented this name for itself, its reversion to mathematics remains integral to it. In the discourse on philosophy that forms the center of Plato's *Republic*, the longest stretch along the way to philosophical knowledge, to ἐπιστήμη, is that which runs through the mathematical disciplines. Both mathematics and ἐπιστήμη—that is, what comes to be called *scientia*, science—belong to the way traversed by and to philosophy. Even though each is set within its proper limits, neither mathematics nor science falls outside of philosophy.

And yet, more recently—so it is said—the sciences, with their bond to mathematics, have gradually separated themselves entirely from philosophy and, in effect, have taken over the investigation of all regions of phenomena. Abandoned to itself, forfeiting perhaps its very name, philosophy must seek out another beginning in which mathematics and science would, it seems, have no place at all. On the one hand, philosophy risks both abstractness from all that was once displayed to those rapt with wonder; and, at the same time, it relies on figures or metaphors drawn directly from this region. On the other hand, philosophy recoils upon science and insists on its diagnosis, namely, that despite science's claim to be based on a rigorous appeal to experience, it is always governed by an unquestioned, antecedent projection of the nature of those things it sets out to investigate. Thus, far from yielding rigorous results, science is burdened, conditioned, by this prior projection presupposed by all its investigations. Such is, then, the state of things: oblivious to the rigor of mathematical thinking, philosophy (or its successor) drifts into abstract metaphoricity, while science, though appropriating mathematics, remains entangled in its compromising presuppositions. There can be no meeting—so it is said—between philosophy and mathematical science, no dialogue in which, most notably, science would offer findings that could be taken up thoughtfully by philosophy.

And yet, even without returning to the ancients' wonder before the natural elements, there prove to be scientific findings that unquestionably are not conditioned by a prior projection, the effect of which would justify philosophy's simply taking its distance. When Galileo, using the recently invented telescope, observed the moons of Jupiter and thereby established that not all heavenly bodies revolve around the earth, this discovery was not conditioned by some prior projection, for indisputably there are moons of Jupiter revolving around the giant planet. Even when Hubble, using the newly installed 100-inch telescope at the Mount Wilson Observatory and relying to an extent on certain mathematical developments, discovered that there are other galaxies beyond the Milky Way, this result was not tainted by some prior projection; for there are, in fact, other galaxies, indeed, by current estimates, ten billion galaxies.

What is thus called for is to break through the wall that has been constructed to separate philosophy from mathematical science. This requires that certain observational findings as well as theoretical results be brought to bear on philosophical interrogations. There is perhaps no better way to begin than to return to the ancients for whom there was no such separation and to orient this return to the spectacle that most of all evoked wonder as that with which philosophy begins—the spectacle of the starry heaven, of the cosmos, and of the time embodied in all that moves across the sky.

If the expression *cosmic time* were to be inscribed in the text of Plato's *Timaeus*, it would be thoroughly tautological. Within Timaeus' discourse—the first of his three discourses—it would be imperative to assert that time belongs to the cosmos in some determinate manner. Quite apart from this time of the cosmos, there is—in an attenuated sense of the copula—that which earthbound mortals believe to be time and which they purport to measure by the use of clocks. Yet, even to apply to this phantom the name *time* is to wander needlessly across the expanse of deceitful δόξαι

The tautology is not one of attribution, as though it prescribed merely, solely, that time belongs to the cosmos. Rather, it is a tautology of identity, a tautology in the strictest sense: not only is time *of* the cosmos but, more specifically and precisely, it is nothing other than the cosmos. To say *time* is to say the same as *cosmos*.

And yet, this is other than what has been said ever since late antiquity, since the era of Middle Platonism, though not prior to that era, neither by Plato's successors in the Academy nor even by Plutarch. What has been said, what has become almost pure dogma, is that time is the moving image of eternity; along with this identification it is assumed that eternity refers to a present that never passes, an eternal presence, *aeternitas* as Augustine terms it. Yet, because the identification of time as the moving image of eternity in this sense has, from Plotinus on, become more and more deeply sedimented, it is exceedingly difficult to unearth it and put it again in question. In order to break through the hardened shell in which it has been encased and simply handed down as such, it is necessary to return to the passage in which Timaeus speaks of time and eternity.

In general, the passage describes certain deeds by the god, who is also called by the name δημιουργός (maker, artisan).[1] At the point in the discourse where the passage occurs, Timaeus has already described how the artisan god produced both the body and the soul of the cosmos. The passage is very brief. Timaeus says:

---

1. See, for example, Plato, *Timaeus*, 28a.

εἰκὼ δ' ἐπινοεῖ κινητόν τινα αἰῶνος ποιῆσαι, καὶ διακοσμῶν ἅμα οὐρανὸν ποιεῖ μένοντος αἰῶνος ἐν ἑνὶ κατ'ἀριθμὸν ἰοῦσαν αἰώνιον εἰκόνα, τοῦτον ὃν δὴ χρόνον ὠνομάκαμεν.

Literally translated the passage reads: "The thought occurs to him of making a moving image of eternity; and in ordering the heaven he, at once, makes the heaven as an image of the eternity that abides in unity, an image moving according to eternal number, that which we call time."[2]

Though a more extended commentary is called for, let me mention only a few points.

1. Note carefully what the opening clause does not say. Though it introduces the phrase "a moving image of eternity," it leaves entirely open the question as to whether it refers to time or to something else. It says only that the god had the thought of making such an image.

2. Forms of the word αἰών, translated as eternity, occur three times in the passage. The word can signify someone's life or lifetime—as when, in the *Odyssey*, a nymph approaches the grieving, homesick Odysseus and, imploring him not to let his life (αἰών) pine away, not to let his lifetime be cut short, promises to send him on his way back to Ithaca.[3] The word can also mean an indefinitely long period of time—as when, in Hesiod's *Theogony*, it is observed that if a man has troublesome children, he will have grief in his heart for a long time (αἰῶνος).[4] Thus, it is by no means necessary that the word be translated, without further ado, as eternity, and most certainly not as aeternitas in the sense of eternal presence. The most appropriate way of determining its sense is by reference to the passage itself: it is a matter of the αἰών that "abides in unity [μένοντος . . . ἐν ἑνὶ]"—that is, that remains within oneness, that remains one and the same as itself, perpetually selfsame.

3. The passage mentions two deeds performed by the god. The first is an ordering, a setting in order. The word is a participial form of διακοσμέω and thus bears a relation to the word κόσμος. In fact, the original sense of κόσμος was (in Homer, for instance) an order or array (as of men going into battle); only because of the order observed in the heaven (οὐρανός), in the movements of the stars, did the word

---

2. Ibid., 37d. The passage is discussed in greater detail in my book *Chorology: On Beginning in Plato's "Timaeus"* (Bloomington: Indiana University Press, 1999), 78–85.
3. Homer, Odyssey, 5.160.
4. Hesiod, *Theogony*, 609.

κόσμος eventually become (as in Plato) almost synonymous with the word οὐρανός (heaven). The other deed is a making, which matches the designation of the god as an artisan. The traditional reading is that what the god *sets in order* is the heaven and that what he *makes* is the image of eternity, that is, time. Yet, recent research[5] supports the thesis that this part of the passage should be rendered: in ordering the heaven, he makes the heaven. This thesis is also supported by the word ἅμα (at once, at the same time), which occurs between the words for ordering and for making. Granted this thesis, it follows that what the god makes is the heaven, not a distinct image that would then be identified as time. Rather, the word *image*, in the phrase "an image of the eternity that abides in unity," explicates the character of the heaven as made by the god.

4. But how does the god make the heaven? What is the character of this making? And what is the relation between the heaven and the cosmos? When the god sets about making the heaven, he has already made both the body of the heaven, most notably its upper fiery part, and its soul, which consists of invisible circles that he has set revolving. When—as described in the present passage—the god makes the heaven, he has only to fashion the heavenly bodies and set them in the orbits already determined by the circles. By setting them in these orbits so that they move in an orderly manner, the god sets the heaven in order. Thus, in making the heaven, the god also sets the heaven in order; indeed he orders it in the very making. Hence, the making and the ordering belong together as a single deed. Furthermore, because in making the heaven it is set *in order*, the word κόσμος, indicative of order, becomes virtually synonymous with οὐρανός (heaven).

5. So, the image that the god makes is the starry heaven, the assemblage of stars in their ordered movement. But how is this an image? Of what is it an image? Earlier in the course of production, when the god made the invisible circles in the cosmic soul, these circles were made in accord with the noetic, perpetually selfsame order, that is, in accord with the eternity that abides in unity. When the god sets the heavenly bodies into these invisible orbits, he produces thereby a *visible* image of that same order, that is, of the eternity that abides in unity. This visible image—the heaven with its revolving bodies—moves in an orderly way, that is according to the very basis and measure of order, that is, according

---

5. See the account in Remí Brague, *Du Temps chez Platon et Aristote* (Paris: Presses Universitaires de France, 1982), 44–46.

to noetic, eternal, selfsame number. What the god thus makes, precisely in ordering it, is the heaven as an image of the eternity that abides in unity, an image moving according to eternal number. Timaeus says that this is what we call time.

6. Thus, finally, it can indeed be said that time is an image of eternity. But this identification does not mean that time is a kind of disembodied specter accompanying visible things; time is not being portrayed as a ghost that hovers over things so as to keep them in order and let them be numbered. On the contrary, time is the same as the starry heaven. It is the embodied movement of the heaven as governed by number. Yet, precisely because it embodies order, the heaven is identical with the cosmos, and time is thus nothing other than the cosmos. The expression cosmic time is a tautology of identity.

Toward the end of Timaeus' first discourse, the figure of cosmic time is again taken up, though in response to a question not previously addressed in the dialogue. The question is simply: What is to be gained by vision of the heaven? Timaeus declares that sight is the cause of the greatest benefit for us. What is this greatest benefit that is conferred by sight? Timaeus answers: "None of the discourse we are now giving about the all [i.e., about the universe—περὶ τοῦ παντός] would ever have been uttered if we had seen neither the stars nor the sun nor the heaven."[6] In effect, Timaeus is declaring that the entire discourse he has given would not have been possible without vision of the heaven and the heavenly bodies. Most remarkably, he identifies the requisite objects of vision not simply as heavenly bodies, not simply as the sun and stars, but rather as the determinations of time that are bound to the movement of the heavenly bodies. Thus, he mentions day and night, the months and the circuits of the year, and the equinoxes and solstices. By vision of these embodiments of time in the heaven, we came, he says, to ponder time as such. In addition, such vision led us to consider number and thus to inquire into the nature of the all (περὶ . . . τῆς τοῦ παντὸς φύσεως). In other words, as Timaeus finally declares: such vision of time embodied in the heaven is what granted us philosophy. The origin of philosophy lies in the vision—presumably a wondrous vision—of the heaven and of the embodiments of time to be seen there.

There are numerous other passages in the *Timaeus* that have a bearing on the figure of cosmic time. One of the most fantastical

---

6. Plato, *Timeaus*, 47a.

describes a celestial choral dance. In virtually every πόλις, choral dances (χορεία) were performed in connection with drama. At the Great Dionysia is Athens, choric dances accompanied both tragedy and comedy; the dancers were chosen by the Archon Eponymos. In each instance the most outstanding dancer was awarded a prize, either a tripod or a tablet commemorating his victory.

But the choral dance that Timaeus describes is set in the starry heaven, and the dancers are themselves the stars—visible, generated gods—specifically those that wander in contrast to those that revolve in uniform motion. As they dance they are sometimes juxtaposed, and at other times they turn back upon the very line of their progression, coming into conjunction with or opposition to each other. If imitations were at hand, one could tell "how they pass behind and in front of each other and at what time (κατὰ χρόνους) each of them is hidden from our view and upon reappearing "send portents of things to come afterwards."[7] Dancing to the rhythm of time, they give signs of what is to come in the time to come. Yet, since time is the same as the starry heaven, their dance is a dance of time.

Yet, the single most impenetrable discourse is that which occupies most of Timaeus' second discourse, the chorology. In this discourse, which undermines itself, turning into a bastard discourse, Timaeus carries out a turn back to that which precedes and is presupposed by the cosmos as made and ordered by the god. Since time is nothing other than the cosmos, Timaeus' retreat is to another time that would be anterior to cosmic time. This time, the time of the χώρα, would be precosmic time, a time before time.

In *Being and Time* Heidegger submits the concept of time to discursive, yet phenomenological interrogation in numerous ways methodologically and in various connections within the overall structure of his project. From these discourses let me extract only the two that bear most closely on the themes that have now emerged as regards cosmic time.

The first of these discourses is of such comprehensiveness that it embraces the entire project. Not only does it commence at the very outset, but also it is the discourse that most decisively interrupted at the

---

7. Ibid., 40c–d.

point where, after the first two Divisions, *Being and Time* breaks off, leaving in abeyance the third Division in which the entire systematic project would have been brought to completion.

At the beginning of *Being and Time*, on the untitled first page, Heidegger writes that his intention is to work out concretely the question of the meaning or sense of being (*die Frage nach dem Sinn von Sein*). In this connection it is imperative to observe that Heidegger's intention is not merely to identify or determine being in its differentiation from beings. His theme is not—contrary to what he sometimes seems to suggest—the so-called ontological difference, that is, the difference between being and beings. As his later writings make explicit, such mere determination of being is precisely what has been carried out repeatedly throughout the history of metaphysics: being has been determined as ἰδέα, as ἐνέργεια, as transcendental subjectivity, as spirit, and so on. Even in *Being and Time*—if less explicitly than later—Heidegger's aim is to advance beyond such determinations to that which, while remaining largely unthought, enables such determinations to be made. In *Being and Time* the name of this "beyond" is *Sinn* (meaning), and the aim is to display phenomenologically—that is, to wrest from concealment—the meaning of being.

Yet, what is meaning—leaving aside the complications that arise from the instability of the question, from the recoil by which it undermines itself? Above all, it is not an idea in the classical sense; it is not set over against, apart from, that of which it is the meaning. Neither is the meaning of something a concept abstracted from it. Rather, it is the horizon—in the phenomenological sense—from which, through reference back from which, something becomes understandable. More precisely meaning is the horizon within which something is set in such a way that from and through the horizon it can be understood. A very concrete example is that of a tool, which in its character as a tool, as functioning in a certain way in the fabrication of something—and not just as a mere thing—is determined by the array of materials, other tools, a workshop, an artisan in which it is situated.

To work out concretely—that is, phenomenologically—the question of the meaning of being is, then, to take up the question of the horizon from which being becomes understandable. Heidegger's problematic is not structured merely by two terms and the difference between them but rather by three terms bound together by the possibility of understanding.

At the very beginning of *Being and Time*—again, on the untitled first page—Heidegger identifies this horizon: "The interpretation of time"—Heidegger writes *time, Zeit*, in italics—"as the possible horizon for every understanding of being as such is the preliminary aim [of this work]."[8] Thus, it is from time that being becomes understandable. Since philosophy has hitherto devoted itself to the understanding of being (as ἰδέα, as ἐνέργεια, etc.), it is time that has, though covertly, rendered this understanding possible. Heidegger's aim is to advance beyond this covert operation of time, to uncover the hidden source—the horizon, that is, time—from which the understanding of being has come about. In both cases it is time that grants the very possibility of philosophy. Though no longer—at least not in this connection—identified with the heaven, the granting otherwise corresponds to that described in the *Timaeus*: in both cases it is through an orientation to time that philosophy is granted. In the one case, this orientation to time takes the form of attentiveness to time in its identity with the cosmos; in the other case, the orientation consists in the envisioning of time as the horizon within which the understanding of being can proceed.

To an extent this parallel may appear overly abstract, especially from Heidegger's side. Yet, in *Being and Time* there is another, very different discourse on time in which the account comes much closer to that in the *Timaeus*.

In the final chapter of the second Division, hence, the final chapter in the book as published, Heidegger describes a certain reckoning or circumspective concern with time that is turned concretely to things. Through this reckoning things are experienced as "within time." This time of within-timeness (*Innerzeitigkeit*) represents an advance toward the constitution of public time or world-time. Yet, a further step is necessary: it lies in the kind of concern that Heidegger describes as the "concern with time that we know as astronomical and calendrical time-reckoning."[9]

Heidegger's description of this kind of concern takes as its point of departure the thrownness of Dasein. As thrown into a setting in which there is alternation of day and night, of illumination and darkness, Dasein is submitted to the rising and setting of the sun, which,

---

8. Martin Heidegger, *Sein und Zeit* (Tübingen: Niemeyer, 1960), 1. Originally published in 1927.

9. Ibid., 411.

says Heidegger, determines "the 'most natural' measure of time—the day." He adds: the dividing up of the day, its articulation into intervals of time, is "carried out with regard to that by which time is dated—the journeying sun."[10] It is this dating—carried out from the heavenly bodies in their distinctive places in the sky—that renders time public so that all come to share it "under the same sky."[11] Most pointedly, in words that could almost be inscribed in the *Timaeus*, Heidegger writes: "'Time' first shows itself in the sky, that is, precisely there where one comes across it in directing oneself naturally *according to it*, so that time even becomes identified with the sky."[12]

For the ancients the cosmos is nothing other than the sky, except that it might be regarded as including also the earth. Yet, reference to the sky already virtually includes reference to the earth from which there is vision of the sky. Thus, to identify time with the sky is to determine it as cosmic time.

With the onset of modernity such identification can no longer be sustained. From Heidegger's identification of time—at least of public time—with the sky, a transition to cosmic time cannot be carried out. The description of time as measured from the sky portrays both time and the sky as they are presented to natural, unaided vision. Yet, in the wake of the discoveries with which what comes to be called modern science begins—most notably the Copernican thesis and Galileo's discoveries—the sky dissolves, as it were, into the cosmos. While at the level of practical life humans continue to take the sun, in its daily journey across the sky, to be the natural measure of time, for the vision that extends beyond, the vision to which there is no such thing as the sky, cosmic time is utterly dissociated from uranic time. Time is no longer restricted to the celestial dome that arches over the earth. Time does not adhere only to the starry heaven.

Along with the dissolution of the sky into the cosmos, there occurs a decentering of the very basis from which the sky and its time had previously been observed. It was decisively established that the earth is not the center of the universe, around which all other celestial bodies would revolve. The decentering of the human vantage point commenced

---

10. Ibid., 412f.
11. Ibid., 413.
12. Ibid., 419.

with the recognition that the earth revolves around the sun, rather than conversely. Yet, this was only the beginning: in its wake came the recognition that the solar system is not the center, not even at the center, of the Milky Way galaxy and that our sun is a rather average star located just off a spur of one of the spiral arms of the galaxy. With Hubble's discovery that there are other galaxies and the eventual realization that there are billions of galaxies, it became ever more evident that there could be no determination of a center, no measure by which to determine a center. To this extent there is justification for declaring that there is no center, not stable point around which the entire cosmos would be ordered.

Even in scientific discourse, there remain—not insignificantly—traces of the time-reckoning that takes the sun, in its daily and annual course, as the natural measure of time; these traces extend to other celestial phenomena such as constellations. Distances to stars are usually expressed using light-years as the measure; and the location where stars are to be seen is often indicated by reference to a constellation—to which of course the star has no relation whatsoever. Yet, to restrict philosophical analysis to consideration only of beings situated on the earth or in the sky can now only appear as provincial. For the existence of other galaxies, for instance, is not a hypothesis based on a prior, hence presupposed projection; there *are* other galaxies, and they are open to observation by anyone with a sufficiently powerful telescope. To restrict the analysis of time in a similar manner, to restrict it to time measured from the sky, cannot but appear as equally provincial.

Despite the decentering that began with Copernicus and Galileo, there endured for three centuries thereafter a rigorously conceived thesis that something remained invariable, that there was something absolutely determined, something determined as absolute.

The definitive expression of this thesis is formulated in Newton's *Principia*. The full title of this work *Philosophiae Naturalis Principia Mathematica* (*Mathematical Principles of Natural Philosophy*) attests to its being situated prior to any rigid divorce between philosophy and natural science. Throughout the definitions, the scholia, the axioms, and their corollaries, both philosophical and scientific prescriptions and demonstrations are juxtaposed in a continuous discourse. For example, the scholium in which Newton presents the most highly theoretical—that is, philosophical—concepts leads directly into his statement of what we call the law of inertia: "Every body perseveres in its state of being at rest or of moving uniformly straight forward, except insofar as it is compelled to change its state by forces impressed."[13]

Newton presents both time and space as absolute; place and motion can be either absolute or relative depending on whether or not they are determined by absolute time and space. Although there can also be relative time and space, it is absolute time and space that determine this relativity. In the scholium expressing all these determinations, Newton requires only a single sentence in order to express the nature of absolute time: "Absolute, true, and mathematical time, in and of itself and of its own nature, without reference to anything external, flows uniformly and by another name is called endurance."[14] Newton observes that relative, apparent, and common time has a sensible and external measure by means of motion. Such measure is provided by an hour, a day, a month. But these measures and the time they measure are to be distinguished from absolute time, indeed absolutely distinguished. While he grants, on the one hand, that there is perhaps no uniform motion by which absolute time can be measured, he insists, on the other hand, that "the flow of absolute time cannot be changed." He declares that absolute space and, by implication, absolute time have no reference to anything external; absolute time is absolute precisely because it is absolved from dependence on anything external and indeed inaccessible as such insofar as it makes no impression on the senses.[15] Absolute time is an absolutely disembodied time.

Thus, absolute time, along with similarly absolute space, institutes a stability that encompasses all things, thereby limiting the breakdown of the order previously taken to govern everything. And yet, even in Newton's statement regarding the nature of absolute time there is evident a certain instability, a slippage, the threat of circularity. Indeed, there is a double threat. First of all, to say simply that absolute time flows absolutely is to pass over the circumstance that flowing presupposes time: whatever flows, even if uniformly, moves across a certain space in a certain interval of time. Thus, to define absolute time by reference to its flowing is to broach a circularity. Secondly, since absolute time itself makes no impression on the senses (like that of relative forms such as an

---

13. Isaac Newton, *Philosophical Writings*, ed. Andrew Janiak (Cambridge: Cambridge University Press, 2004), 70. Newton's *Principia* was originally published in 1687.
14. Ibid., 64.
15. Ibid., 66–69.

hour or a day), it can announce itself only through motion that occurs in it. Yet, not only does Newton admit that "it is possible that there is no uniform motion by which time [he means here *absolute* time] may have an exact measure"[16]; but also this connection too, the connection between absolute time and motion borders on circularity, for motion is always motion *in time*.

Already with Newton, the stable basis provided by absolute, disembodied time begins—short of a theological appeal—to show signs of dissolution. Yet, the decisive blow to it comes in the early twentieth century. In fact, it is a double blow, both at the theoretical level and at the level of astronomical observation.

At the theoretical level the absoluteness of time and of space is undermined by the special theory of relativity. Minimally expressed, the primary result of this theory can be illustrated as follows. If there are two bodies, K and K′, with Cartesian coordinate systems (that is, x-, y-, and z-axes, mutually perpendicular), and if K′ is in motion along the x-axis of K, then the time when an event happens with respect to K′ does not simply coincide with the time when it happens with respect to K. This difference depends on the movement along the spatial x-axis and can be calculated using the Lorentz transformation equation. As a result the strict separation of time from space is disrupted. By coupling time and space in this manner, the special theory of relativity cancels the absoluteness of each.

However, in Einstein's view this result does not entirely disrupt Newtonian absoluteness; it merely transfers it from space and time taken separately to the coupling, which he designates simply as space-time. Einstein states this conclusion explicitly, and then, quite significantly, he writes that absoluteness "means not only 'physically real,' but also 'independent in its physical properties, having a physical effect, but not itself influenced by physical conditions.'"[17] Thus, in the special theory of relativity, just as with Newton, space and time, though now coupled, are immune to any effect by the bodies that occur in them. As coupled, they remain disembodied.

---

16. Ibid., 66.
17. Albert Einstein, *The Meaning of Relativity*, 4th ed. (Princeton: Princeton University Press, 1953), 55.

Only in the general theory of relativity, which is essentially a theory of gravitation, do space and time regain their embodiment. For, according to this theory—repeatedly confirmed by observation—space-time is distorted, stretched, around large bodies such as stars; that is, space-time proves not to be immune to effects by the bodies that occur in it. And yet, here again there is a threat of circularity as soon as the transition is made from mathematical elaboration to physical description; and it begins to seem as though circularity were almost intrinsic to the endeavor to determine the nature of time and space. For distortion and stretching occur *in* space-time, which cannot, then, be simply determined by these features.

At the level of observation there are results that, though not entirely contrary to Newtonian theory, do seriously alter the general outlook accompanying this theory. These results, established through modern astrophysical research, have been greatly amplified since Hubble's discovery that there are other galaxies beyond the Milky Way, galaxies that are almost unimaginably distant from the human point of observation on the earth. The most decisive result is that in the case of such distant stars, and even with stars in the Milky Way, there is no simultaneity between observation and that which is observed, between seeing and the seen. What one sees when looking through a telescope at a star—or, for instance, at the Andromeda Galaxy, which, though 2.5 million light-years away, is the nearest galaxy to the Milky Way—is not that star or galaxy as it is in our present, at the present moment when on looks through the telescope, but rather as it was in a remote past—in the case of the Andromeda Galaxy, as it was 2.5 million years ago. In such cases there is a separation of time from itself, an enormous gap between the present of the seeing and the present of the seen. In other words, what is given to sensible intuition is not something present but something long since past. There is a decisive breach between intuition and presence.

The decisiveness of this breach becomes evident in view of the rigorous correlation that Heidegger has traced throughout the entire history of metaphysics, the correlation between intuition and presence: what one sees in the present is something present, something present in its presence. Even in cases where, as with certain philosophers such as Kant, intuition alone is insufficient and requires a supplement, the basic correlation remains in effect. Even if supplemented, for instance, by understanding, intuition is intuition of presence; and metaphysics, appropriating this correlation, is metaphysics of presence. In his own thinking, Heidegger sets out to surpass this correlation, to get over—or rather, under—the metaphysics of presence, to do so by exposing what remains unthought in the metaphysical correlation of intuition and presence. In this regard his task becomes that of uncovering the coming to presence that makes possible the correlation but that also holds back, preventing that which comes to presence from exposing itself without reserve. The parallel goes only so far, but it is nonetheless a parallel: as the object retreats from presence to intuition, so a distant celestial object holds itself back from the earthbound observer, showing only its remote past.

The correlation between intuition and presence is brought into question, perhaps even more decisively, by Derrida. In his deconstruction of the Husserlian phenomenology of time-consciousness, Derrida demonstrates that there is no pure present, no *lebendige Gegenwart*, as Husserl calls it. Rather, according to Derrida's analysis, the very constitution of the present involves the retended. In other words, it is not that the present is first constituted as such and then, as it were, extends into the immediate past by means of retention. Rather, the past enters into the very constitution, the very upsurge, of the present.

In the case of Derrida the astronomical parallel is still closer. Just as, according to Derrida's analysis, the past is, in a constitutive sense, brought into the present, so in astronomical observation the past of a celestial object is brought into the present of the observation. In both cases the intrusion of the past is not merely coincidental but occurs, rather, by necessity. Most remarkably, then, there is a certain accord between deconstruction and the findings of modern astrophysics.

Returning, finally, to the *Timaeus*, dreaming of the χώρα, even if in a daydream, stammering in bastardly speech about the time before time in which the χώρα held traces of elements not yet themselves, one can even by these means intimate that the χώρα is at least as withdrawn from presence as are the stars. And just as the past of the stars is brought, as past, into the present, so the χώρα, never abandoning the time before time, enters the presence of the cosmos and grants to the god the ground—or rather, the unground, the abyss—from which can be fashioned the cosmos and the time identical with it.

10 THE NEGATIVITY OF TIME-SPACE

In the title of Heidegger's initial project, the entire course that its demonstrative analyses will traverse is delimited. For it is through the increasingly more explicit analyses of time that the question of the meaning of being comes to be developed. Though time goes largely unconsidered in the articulation of the existentials that constitute the being of Dasein, the unveiling of temporality as their ground is merely deferred. Thus, once the ecstatic character of temporality has been exposed, the analysis of the existentials must be repeated so as to display their grounding in temporality.

It turns out, then, that the progression from being to time has as its complement a regression from time to being. This circle traces the limits of—that is, delimits—Heidegger's initial project in its broadest expanse.

The unveiling of time as grounding the being of Dasein extends, then, from the beginning to the end of *Being and Time*. Yet, in addition, there is to be found at the beginning and at the end, respectively, two unique and very different results that are to be—or that come to be—achieved. At the beginning the result is merely anticipated, namely, in the statement that the preliminary goal of *Being and Time* is the interpretation of time as the horizon of the understanding of being. Since, in the analyses within the work, meaning will be shown to have the character of horizon, this statement is tantamount to declaring that the goal is to interpret time as the meaning of being.

At the other extreme the result is quite different and conveys a sense of time that does not readily cohere with the initial statement. In the final chapter of *Being and Time*, Heidegger describes a certain kind of reckoning with time that contrasts both with the orientation to the question of being and with the analysis of the ecstatic character of time. It is this concrete reckoning that lets things appear as "within time" and that presupposes a concern with time in its astronomical appearance, especially in the rising and setting of the sun, indeed in the entire course followed by the sun, which thus determines the articulation of the day, hence of natural time.[1] Such is the context in which Heidegger puts forth a statement regarding time that appears to fall entirely outside the bounds of his ontological project. Most likely it is this externality, this displacement, that is marked by the reservation with which he writes the word: "'Time' [»*die Zeit*«] first shows itself precisely in the sky, that is, there where one comes across it in directing oneself naturally *according to it*, so that 'time' [»*die Zeit*«] even becomes identified with the sky."[2]

A similar reference is found later in *The Event* (dated 1941–42), though what is referred to is space rather than time. What is especially pertinent is that the reference is again to the sky. Heidegger declares that mundane space—the space occupied by things (*Dingraum*)—"is accessible to us only by way of the space in which the stars exist."[3]

In *Being and Time* the two results regarding time border on opposition, though this opposition is not at all simply symmetrical. On the one hand, time is oriented to being; indeed, as the projected meaning of being, it is cast even beyond being (ἐπέκεινα τῆς οὐσίας).[4] On the other hand, it is referred to beings such as the sun and to the space of such beings, the sky. Time is thus oriented both to being and to beings, in particular, to the space of those beings that we share "under the same sky."[5] To be sure, Heidegger attempts to rein in the latter result, to demonstrate that astronomical time is grounded in ecstatic temporality. Yet, regardless of whether this effort succeeds or not, the results of the analyses serve to pose two comprehensive and fundamental tasks. The reference of time to the space of the heavenly bodies poses the task of thinking through the cohesion of time and space, of doing so in a manner that surpasses Heidegger's effort to found Dasein's spatiality on

---

1. See Martin Heidegger, *Sein und Zeit* (Tübingen: Max Niemeyer, 1960), 411–20 (§80). For a detailed account of this analysis, see above, chap. 9.
2. Heidegger, ibid.
3. Heidegger, *Das Ereignis*, GA 71: 216–17 (§240).
4. See Heidegger, *Die Grundprobleme der Phänomenologie*, GA 24: 404 (§20).
5. Heidegger, *Sein und Zeit*, 413 (§80).

temporality, an effort that he later confesses was inadequate.⁶ But, in turn, in the oppositional relation between the two results there is posed the further task of thinking cohesive time and space in their relation to being, to the meaning of being, to what will come to be thought as the truth of being.⁷

In the thinking that, thus protended, opens beyond *Being and Time*, a decisive—even the most decisive—role is assumed by the concept of negativity, though, in the course of this thinking, negativity will prove to limit the very provenance of the concept as such. Yet, already in *Being and Time* negativity enters into several of the most extensive and fundamental analyses. Three such analyses are especially pertinent.

The first is the analysis of anxiety. Here Heidegger forges a connection between this distinctively disclosive disposition and the experience of the uncanny (*Unheimlichkeit*). Expressing literally a not-being-at-home (*Nicht-zuhause-sein*), the word is taken to signify the indefiniteness in which Dasein finds itself in anxiety, "the nothing and nowhere," as Heidegger calls it.⁸ In being exposed to this nothing and nowhere, Dasein encounters a distinctive mode of negativity.

In the second analysis, that of death, the indication is still more direct. It lays out the various forms in which negativity enters into being-toward-death. The analysis begins with the observation that in death "Dasein is no longer there [*ist . . . zum Nicht-mehr-da-sein geworden*]."⁹ At a deeper level of the analysis, Heidegger describes the character of death in these—so often repeated and recast—words: it is *"the possibility of the impossibility of existence as such."*¹⁰ Most telling is his declara-

---

6. Heidegger, *Zur Sache des Denken*, GA 14: 29.
7. When, in the development that Heidegger's thought undergoes after *Being and Time*, "The question of being becomes the question of the truth of being" (Heidegger, *Beiträge zur Philosophie*, GA 65: 428 [§259]), this task is accordingly transformed. One consequence is that the concept of horizon is subverted. As a result, the question of being can no longer be construed in terms of the manner in which time provides the horizon within which and from which being can be—and always has been—understood and interpreted. Through this development the concept of horizon (which is essentially phenomenological) falls away (see Heidegger, *Aus der Erfahrung des Denkens*, GA 13: 44f.), and the task becomes that of thinking time and space in their emergence within the event of truth.
8. Heidegger, *Sein und Zeit*, 188 (§40).
9. Ibid., 236 (§46).
10. Ibid., 262 (§53).

tion that death, as a possibility to which, from birth, Dasein comports itself, gives Dasein *nothing*—nothing that it could aim at actualizing, nothing even that one could imagine actualizing. Being-toward-death gives *nothing*; it is pure negativity.

A decade later, in *Contributions to Philosophy*, Heidegger radicalizes the connection between being-toward-death and negativity, while, in this very move, he broaches a concurrence of negativity and being, which by then will have proved to constitute the center—if there be a center—of his discourse. He declares that one of the fundamental determinations harbored in being-toward-death is that in it "there is concealed the essential belongingness of the nothing to being as such."[11]

The analysis of being-toward-death developed in *Being and Time* already tacitly reveals a connection between negativity and time. For the projection upon death as possibility is, like all projective understanding, grounded on temporality. Hence, the negativity that haunts being-toward-death leads back to temporality as its ground.

In the third of the analyses, that of guilt, Heidegger displays still more openly the specific form in which negativity enters into this phenomenon. He declares that in the very idea of guilt "there lies the character of the *not*."[12] More specifically, he writes: "we determine the formal existential idea of 'guilty' as: being the ground of a being [*Sein*] that is determined by a not—that is, *being the ground of a negativity* [*Grundsein einer Nichtigkeit*]."[13] In the course of the analysis that follows, Heidegger identifies the ways in which, both in understanding and as thrown, necessarily guilty Dasein is the ground of a negativity. In understanding, a projection on certain possibilities entails that other possibilities are excluded, negated—that Dasein does *not* take up these other possibilities. In its thrownness, the negativity lies in Dasein's inability to bring itself into its Da, that it cannot come back behind its thrownness so as to release from itself its being-thrown. In other words, the *Da* exceeds the range of what Dasein can take in hand and control.

Since in and through its constitutive moments Dasein is intrinsically guilty, negativity proves to be operative at its very core. Thus it is that Heidegger goes on to attribute negativity to care as such, that is, to the very being of Dasein. He is explicit, indeed emphatic: "*Care itself, in*

---

11. Heidegger, *Beiträge zur Philosophie*, GA 65: 282 (§160).
12. Heidegger, *Sein und Zeit*, 283 (§58).
13. Ibid.

THE NEGATIVITY OF TIME-SPACE   157

its essence, is permeated through and through with negativity." Still more directly, more explicitly, he writes that care "means . . . : being the (negative) ground of a negativity."[14] Furthermore, since temporality is the ontological meaning of care—the meaning of the being of Dasein—temporality cannot be devoid of the negativity that permeates care. Negativity cannot but be intrinsic to time.

Following the analysis by which is exposed the negativity within guilt and within care, there is a remarkable series of admissions and questions by which Heidegger attests to the incompleteness of his analysis. He grants that "the ontological meaning of the notness [*Nichtheit*] of this existential negativity [*Nichtigkeit*] remains obscure."[15] More expansively, he declares that the ontological essence of the *not* in general remains obscure. There follows a series of questions that effectively extend the range of the interrogation that needs to be brought to bear on negativity. Is it obvious, Heidegger asks, that every negative has the sense of a lack and that what positivity it has goes no further than the mere idea of passing over something null and void? In other words, is it obvious that in negating something one marks it as a nullity and through the negation passes on beyond it to something else? Equally protentious is Heidegger's reference to dialectic. Why is it, he asks, that dialectic constantly resorts to the negative without, however, being able to ground it dialectically? Here Heidegger's encounter with Hegel appears on the horizon. In that encounter he will take up the very questions that he will have posed in *Being and Time* regarding negativity.

In Heidegger's 1929 inaugural lecture *What Is Metaphysics?*, he takes up again the question of negativity, traversing along somewhat different lines much of the same terrain as in the corresponding analyses in *Being and Time*. Especially prominent is the account of anxiety as the attunement in which Dasein is brought, in the starkest manner, before the nothing. The lecture also recasts the description of the being of Dasein—that is, of care—as permeated with negativity. In this regard Heidegger writes: "Da-sein means: being held out into the nothing."[16]

The most conspicuous advance in the lecture is broached by Heidegger's contention that, were Dasein not held out into the nothing, it

---

14. Ibid., 285 (§58).
15. Ibid.
16. Heidegger, *Wegmarken*, GA 9: 115.

could never be related to beings or even to itself. In other words—words that indeed leap ahead—"The nothing is what makes possible the openness of beings as such for Dasein."[17] In words that leap even farther ahead: the nothing is not merely the indeterminate opposite of beings but "reveals itself as belonging to the being of beings."[18] Heidegger's account entails that the nothing—that is, negativity—is not the opposite either of beings or of being itself. Rather than being the opposite of being—even in the dialectical sense—negativity belongs to being. Now, even more prominently, Hegel comes upon the scene. It is highly appropriate that at precisely this point Heidegger cites from Hegel's *Logic*, namely, the statement that being and nothing are the same. Needless to say, everything depends on the sense assumed by the word *same*.

Heidegger's encounter with Hegel regarding negativity is inscribed in a text from 1938–39 entitled "*Negativity: A Confrontation with Hegel Approached from Negativity*."[19] Heidegger's strategies in this text are to some degree governed by his acute awareness that any opposition to Hegel's system risks becoming merely symmetrical therewith, in which case it cannot avoid being reabsorbed into the system. In the case most significant for Heidegger, the counter position cannot succeed by positing being and nothing as opposites, counter to Hegel's assertion that being and nothing are the same. For in Hegel's *Logic* this assertion comes about as the *Aufhebung* of the assertion that they are opposed. Since the assertion of opposition is, as *aufgehoben*, nonetheless preserved in the dialectical result, it is already incorporated into the system. In other words what would be put forth as counter to Hegel's system would be absorbed into the system and its character as counter to the system would be negated, suspended.

Heidegger grants that within Hegel's system negativity is the basic determination. He echoes Hegel's own assertion of "the enormous power of the negative," that it is "the energy of thought."[20] On the other hand, Heidegger charges that in the system there is "complete dissolution into the positivity of the absolute."[21] In Hegel's terms it is a matter

---

17. Ibid., *GA* 9: 115
18. Ibid., *GA* 9: 120.
19. Heidegger, *Hegel*, *GA* 68: 1–60.
20. G. W. F. Hegel, *Phänomenologie des Geistes*, vol. 9 of *Gesammelte Werke* (Hamburg: Felix Meiner, 1980), 27.
21. Ibid., 14.

of determinate negation, of negation that, in being itself negated, is transformed into positivity. The reiteration of such transformation defines the life of spirit, which is described in one of the most decisive and oft-cited passages in the Preface to the *Phenomenology of Spirit*. The passage reads: Spirit "is this power only by looking the negative in the face and tarrying with it. This tarrying [with the negative] is the magical power [*die Zauberkraft*] that converts it into being."[22]

Heidegger does not directly oppose Hegel's dissolution of negativity into positivity. He does not risk staking out a position that would then prove to be reabsorbed into the system. Rather, his opposition is oblique in that both being and the negative are fundamentally redetermined. As such they coincide, and to this extent there is an affinity with Hegel's assertion that being and nothing are the same. Yet, their coincidence is of an entirely different sort. The difference stems from the determination of negativity as abyss. Heidegger writes the word in hyphenated form, as *Ab-grund*, in order to express its coincidence with ground, that is, with being. Thus, he asserts that the most a-byssal (*das Ab-gründigste*) is being itself. In order to express the mutation that being undergoes through its conjunction with the abyssal, he writes it in the form *Seyn*.

On the other hand, Heidegger asserts that negativity as abyss is opposed to beyng, that it is the abyssal contrary of beyng. And yet, he adds immediately that abyssal negativity, in its very difference from beyng, is the essence of being. In these assertions he opposes Hegel's position that being and nothing are the same. Yet, this opposition is oblique rather than symmetrical. Being and the abyssal nothing are opposed; there is between them a difference that cannot be dialectically surpassed. And yet, in this very difference, they coincide, they are the same.

How, then, if not dialectically, do being and nothing—in their identity and difference—belong together?

The abyss—that is, negativity—is nothing other than the ground, nothing set apart from it. It is through its grounding that there is opened a clearing (*Lichtung*) in which beings can come to be present. Yet, precisely as abyssal, the ground is never itself present; it refuses itself, withdraws, in the very grounding that clears a space for beings. It is abyssal and yet it grounds. This abyss that belongs essentially to the ground is the negativity intrinsic to ground; it is the negativity that belongs to beyng. Beyng and nothing are neither the same nor different. Rather,

---

22. Ibid.

the nothing is, as it were, coiled within beyng in such a way as to render beyng itself abyssal.

In thinking the abyss of beyng, Heidegger thinks negativity in a way that escapes the reach of dialectic and that carries it beyond metaphysics as such.

How does negativity, redetermined in this way, bear on space and time? Can Heidegger's rethinking of negativity serve to launch the kind of inquiry prompted by Heidegger's referring of time to the sky, to the space of the heavenly bodies? Can the redetermination of negativity as abyss provide a means by which to extend ontologically the connection between negativity and time revealed in the analyses of being-toward-death and of guilt and care?

In *Contributions to Philosophy*, which was composed a decade after *Being and Time* and at virtually the same time as the text on Hegel, Heidegger devotes an entire section to the question of space and time. This section falls within the fugal division entitled "The Grounding." In the title of this section, the hyphenated word *Ab-grund* occurs.[23] These indications serve to portend that the account of the abyssal ground forged through the encounter with Hegel will figure prominently in the determinations of space and time undertaken in *Contributions to Philosophy*.

Heidegger poses the question: Why, ever since antiquity, have space and time been thought together? Why, conceived, for instance, as kinds of order or as schemata,[24] have they always been yoked together, since they are radically different and indeed have nothing whatsoever in common? Why space *and* time? Heidegger takes the "and" as his clue: the "and" that conjoins space and time points back to the ground of the essence of both. In order to think them in their essential conjunction, it is necessary—says Heidegger—to dislodge or derange them (the word is *Verrückung*, a noun form of *verrückt*, which means *mad* or *crazy*). Thereby they are brought back, resituated, within the open (*das Offene*), within the clearing, within the sphere of ἀλήθεια. It is here that they have their common essence. Though throughout the history of metaphysics they were always regarded as conjoined, their common essence could—Heidegger contends—never be thought because the locus of their

---

23. The full title is *Der Zeitraum als der Ab-grund*.
24. The references are to Leibniz and Kant, respectively.

commonality, ἀλήθεια, had been abandoned and replaced by ὁμοίωσις. In the first beginning the essential "and" gave way to an "and" that only indicated from afar the essential conjunction of space and time.

Heidegger proposes to recover and redetermine this essential conjunction of space and time by thinking them as originally united in what he terms, in hyphenated form, *time-space* (*Zeit-Raum*). He designates time-space as the "common root" of space and time.[25]

The entire discourse on time-space focuses on the bond between time-space and the essence of truth. In fact, the immediately preceding section of *Contributions to Philosophy* is devoted to an analysis of the essence of truth. This section takes over and extends the analysis of truth in Heidegger's earlier text *On the Essence of Truth* (first composed in 1930). Most significantly, it takes over from the earlier text the deconstruction of the opposition between truth and untruth; in that text Heidegger shows that untruth is not simply the opposite of truth but rather belongs to truth. In addition, truth is itself redetermined as disclosedness, as unconcealing; since it is precisely in and as the open—that is, the clearing—that unconcealing takes place, truth can also be determined as clearing—or, recovering the ancient sense, as ἀλήθεια.

In *On the Essence of Truth* a certain strategy is employed, one that recurs decisively in later texts. It can readily be discerned in Heidegger's confrontation with Hegel, in his move from the sheer opposition between being and nothing (such that their identity can supervene dialectically) to a configuration in which this opposition is deconstructed through the inclusion of one opposite within the other, that is, of untruth within truth, of abyss within ground, of negativity within being. Such inclusion does not simply cancel the difference that would obtain if these pairs were opposites; rather, it resituates that difference within the belonging of one would-be opposite to the other. In this strategy, which governs many of Heidegger's analyses—especially where there looms the threat of dialectic—one can discern a kind of logic operative in Heidegger's texts, a logic quite other than the conventional logic of noncontradiction, which has been taken to be logic as such ever since its codification by Aristotle. In Heidegger's strategy there is broached a breakthrough to another logic.

---

25. Heidegger, *Beiträge zur Philosophie*, GA 65: 298 (§241).

In *Contributions to Philosophy* Heidegger takes up the pairing of truth and untruth as clearing and concealing. Yet, since untruth belongs to truth, since it is internal to truth rather than opposed to it, the pairing can be formulated more precisely by supplementing the phrase "clearing and concealing" with the stipulation: as one (concealment) belongs to the other (clearing), or, more comprehensively, as each belongs to the other. This says, on the one side, that in the happening of clearing—that is, of truth—there is also, within that very clearing, concealment. But also, on the other side, in the happening of concealment there is also, interior to it, clearing. Since concealing is always also self-concealing, that is, since concealing conceals itself, it could never become manifest, were it not for the clearing that belongs to it. This pairing, thought radically, Heidegger often formulates in the expression "clearing for concealing" ("*Die Lichtung für die Verbergung*"). Here it becomes evident that in the inclusion there is a kind of reduplication by which that which is included in the other also includes the other within itself; otherwise, clearing could not be readily subordinated to concealment, as in the phrase "clearing for concealment."

In the course of his discourse on truth in *Contributions to Philosophy*, Heidegger ventures even to reformulate the pairing in the phrase "truth is untruth"; he warns, however, that, though it serves the purpose of indicating the strangeness of the determination of truth, this formulation is seductive and easily misunderstood, especially if construed in the direction of Nietzsche's dictum that truth is the error without which a certain kind of living being cannot live. To declare that truth is untruth is of course to undermine that very declaration. The declaration cancels itself, and yet, for Heidegger, it expresses something essential. He writes: "This statement, deliberately formulated to be in conflict with itself, is meant to say expressly that the *negative* [*das Nichthafte*] belongs to truth, but by no means merely as a lack but as resistance, as that self-concealing that comes into the clearing as such."[26] In other words, the concealing that belongs to clearing constitutes the negativity of truth.

By laying out the various determinations of the essence of truth as well as the logic of oppositional inclusion, which is extended from truth to being and to ground, the stage is set for the analysis of time-space. It will be expedient to reconfigure—indeed to structure—this quite

---

26. Ibid., *GA* 65: 356 (§228).

disseminated analysis as proceeding through a series of five stages. These stages do not by any means exhaust the resources of Heidegger's analyses. Several strands of the discourse lead beyond the scope of the present account, perhaps most notably, that by which the thinking of the event (*Ereignis*) is woven into the analysis of time-space. Other concepts that remain subordinate, that are merely broached but left undeveloped—such as that of the "momentary site" (*Augenblicksstätte*)—must also be left aside.

Note, first of all, that the section on time-space begins by positing a certain relatedness between time-space and the essence of truth. Specifically, Heidegger identifies "time-space as arising out of and belonging to the essence of truth."[27] Yet, this arising and belonging are of a unique kind. It is not as if the essence of truth—that is, clearing/concealment—is already in place, already deployed, such that time-space would somehow be generated by and from it and hence would be simply derivative. On the contrary, Heidegger declares that "time-space is merely the essential unfolding of the essential occurrence of truth [*die Wesensentfaltung der Wesung der Wahrheit*]."[28] This says: the essence of truth, its very deployment, occurs through the essential unfolding that takes place as time-space.

The second stage is launched with the question: What form does this deployment, this essential unfolding of truth that takes place as time-space, assume? In other words, what are the joinings, junctures (the word is *Fügung*), that is, the structural moments that are operative in this unfolding? There are two such moments, which Heidegger describes with the words *Entrückung* and *Berückung*. *Entrückung* has the sense of being carried away, removed, transported beyond, as in ecstasy. *Berückung* has the sense of being captivated by what is at hand. The words are of course related to the word *Verrückung*, which, as noted already, has the sense of dislodging or deranging.

The two words, taken together, thus describe the deployment of truth that takes place as time-space, as the conjunction of transport beyond and adherence to what is at hand. In and as the essential unfolding of truth in its essence, these moments happen at once; one could say that they happen at the same time, were it not that this happening

---

27. Ibid., *GA* 65: 371 (§238).
28. Ibid., *GA* 65: 386 (§242).

is antecedent to the emergence of time. Furthermore, through the allusion to *Verrückung*, there is a hint that in this happening there is a dislodging—indeed, a dislodging corresponding to what Heidegger describes as the "dislodging of the essence of the human into Da-sein."[29] One could say: in that the human is engaged in the occurrence of truths in the operation of time-space, the human undergoes such dislodging—that is, becomes deranged, is exposed to μανία, to madness.

At the third stage Heidegger takes up the question of ground in a manner not unlike that in the contemporaneous text on Hegel. Heidegger declares that time-space grounds the "there" (the "*Da*"), the open region in which beings can come to presence. Indeed, he says in this connection that it is through the "there" that selfhood and beings in their truth "first come to be grounded."[30] In other words, in and through the grounding of the "there," that is, the grounding in which is opened the sphere of appearance, both oneself and beings are granted the expanse in which they can come to presence. The very possibility of their appearance thus has time-space as its ground, twice removed.

But what kind of ground is time-space? And how does it ground the "there"? What kind of grounding occurs here?

Heidegger calls it an abyssal grounding. Through time-space there takes place an "abyssal grounding of the 'there.'"[31] Thus, the grounding takes place as abyssal; that is, in the grounding, the grounding occurs as abyss. The abyss, he says, "is the originary essence [*Wesung*] of the ground."[32] This is to say, then, that time-space, as the essential occurrence of truth, as the ground of the "there," is to be grasped as abyssal, as the *Ab-grund* that belongs essentially to the *Grund*. Heidegger consistently hyphenates the word *Ab-grund* in order to stress this belonging of the *Ab-grund* to the *Grund*. The *Ab-grund* is not the opposite of the *Grund* but belongs to it. The abyss is interior to the ground rather than being posed over against it as its opposite. Here again Heidegger's strategy is to deconstruct opposition by turning it into an inclusion, in which, nonetheless, differentiation is retained.

Granted the belonging of abyss to ground, the question is: What is this abyssal occurrence that brings about the very achieving of

---

29. Ibid., *GA* 65: 372 (§239).
30. Ibid., *GA* 65: 376 (§240).
31. Ibid., *GA* 65: 376 (§240).
32. Ibid., *GA* 65: 379 (§242).

grounding? Heidegger describes it as an *Ausbleiben*—a staying away, an absenting—of ground. It is a self-concealing of ground—in Heidegger's words, a "self-concealing in the mode of the refusal [*Versagung*] of the ground."³³ It is the self-withholding of ground.³⁴

But how is it, then, that in and through a withholding of ground there occurs an achieving of grounding? How, if time-space withholds itself, does it ground the "there" and thereby provide an open region in which beings can come to presence? How is it that time-space grounds and yet, since it withdraws, does not properly ground?

Heidegger's response—and nothing is more crucial—is that the self-withholding of ground brings about "a distinctive and originary kind of leaving unfilled-out, of leaving empty." Thereby it accomplishes "a distinctive kind of opening up."³⁵ In other words, by withdrawing from what will be the site of the "there," the ground leaves the site empty, without ground, and precisely thereby it opens up the site. In Heidegger's words: "In withholding itself, the ground preeminently brings into the open, namely, into the first opening of *that* emptiness, which is thereby a determinate one. . . . In this withholding, the originary emptiness opens up and the originary *clearing* occurs."³⁶ Thus, it is the self-withholding abyssal ground that brings about the clearing, that lets it open up at a site. Indeed, the connection is so intimate that by inserting only minimal mediation—namely, the word *erstwesentlich*—Heidegger can declare that the *Ab-grund* is the clearing/concealment, that is, the essence of truth. Yet, this is only "the first clearing," and "it abides in hesitancy [*Zögerung*]." It is such because something further must take place in order that the "there" be fully grounded.

---

33. Ibid., *GA* 65: 380 (§242).
34. It is in this connection that Heidegger abruptly introduces references to what he terms the *Ur-grund* and the *Un-grund*. The extreme compactness of the discourse at this point excludes all but minimal and provisional interpretation. He writes: "The *Ur-grund* [a possible translation is: primordial ground] opens itself, as what is self-concealing, only in the *Ab-grund*." Presumably the *Ur-grund* is to be taken as the ground *as such* ("beyng essentially occurring in its truth"), which, however, as entirely self-concealing, is disclosed only in and through the *Ab-grund*, in which the ground is both concealed and exposed. On the other hand, the *Ab-grund* can itself be completely concealed through what is termed the *Un-grund* (see ibid., *GA* 65: 380 [§242]).
35. Ibid., *GA* 65: 379 (§242).
36. Ibid., *GA* 65: 380 (§242).

At the fourth stage there is a return to the question of time-space, of its emergence as the essential unfolding of the essential occurrence of truth. The question is: How, in and through the withdrawing of the *Ab-grund*, does time-space come into play as the original unity that breaks asunder into time and space? How does time-space come to be installed in the "first clearing" in such a way that the clearing as such is constituted?

Heidegger's response is formulated in a monstrously abyssal, barely penetrable discourse, which thus enacts discursively that to which it is addressed. He focuses again on the self-withdrawing of the ground, which leaves what will be the site of the "there" empty. It is, then, precisely into this emptiness that the various transportings (*Entrückungen*) enter. There is transporting toward—that is, into—the emptiness of what is not-yet, of what is to come; there is transporting toward—that is, into—the emptiness of what is no-longer, of what has passed by. It is the conjunction, the gathering, of these transportings and, in addition, their impact (which "constitutes the present") that constitutes temporalization. Since temporalization is granted—or, more precisely, its site is first opened up—by the self-withholding of the *Ab-grund*, Heidegger declares that the *Ab-grund* grounds in the mode of temporalization. In an allied but distinctive manner, spatialization arises from captivation (*Berückung*), from the entrance of captivation into the empty site opened by the self-withdrawing of ground. It is the unity of such originary temporalization and spatialization that constitutes time-space. The *Ab-grund* grounds as time-space. Thus, time-space is nothing other than the *Ab-grund* as, withdrawingly, it grounds. Hence the title of the entire discourse devoted to time-space: *Der Zeit-Raum als der Ab-grund*.

Heidegger stresses that temporalization and spatialization cannot be understood on the basis of the usual representations of time and space. On the contrary, time and space can be grasped in their very source only from temporalization and spatialization—that is, most originarily, from time-space. Heidegger's account as to how such a derivation would proceed offers only the most preliminary indications, emphasizing that it would require leaving traditional conceptions behind and adhering to the proper conception of time-space.

How, in the end, do time and space come to structure what otherwise would be only the *first* clearing? How, in particular, are they to be thought concretely and not only as remote derivatives from the self-withdrawing of the *Ab-grund*? Heidegger leaves these questions largely

THE NEGATIVITY OF TIME-SPACE   167

unanswered, hardly even posed. But there is one brief passage that in this regard is quite remarkable. Heidegger writes: "Only where something at hand [*ein Vorhandenes*] is seized and determined does there arise the flow of 'time' [»*Zeit*«] that flows by it and the 'space' [»*Raum*«] that surrounds it."[37] A possible interpretation would be: time and space become manifest only in connection with things—as in the case of the "time" that first announces itself in the space of the heavenly bodies.

The final stage of Heidegger's analysis makes explicit the bond between time-space and negativity. Heidegger begins by excluding, or at least qualifying, a certain kind of negativity. He observes that the *Ab-grund* is not the negation of *Grund*. The abyss is no proclamation of unlimited groundlessness. On the contrary, the abyss is an affirmation of ground, since it is precisely through the self-withholding of the abyssal ground that the "there" comes to be grounded. Yet, if considered immediately, both the *Ab-grund* and the refusal or withholding contain a certain negativity, which is thus a negativity of time-space. For the abyss is, in a sense, the negative of ground and the refusal is the negative of bestowal or granting. And yet, in both instances Heidegger's analysis displaces the negativity, breaks down the opposition expressed by negation. For the abyss belongs to the ground rather than being symmetrically opposed to it; and the refusal of ground, rather than negating its bestowal, is the very means by which the bestowal of ground is accomplished. In both cases the alleged negation proves to be interior to, rather than opposed to, its would-be opposite.

Such is the logic of the negativity—that of time-space—that enables the deployment of the essence of truth, that lets a clearing for concealment take place.

And yet, it seems that at a certain juncture this logic is violated. For Heidegger insists that there is a *not* that is neither a mere opposite nor a negativity included in its would-be opposite, a *not* that is not coiled up within that which it would negate. Heidegger calls it "the originary *not*."[38] He identifies it only to the extent of saying that it is the *not* that belongs to beyng itself and thus to the event. Beyond this he says only that this negativity occurs in the withholding. One can only surmise that it is the negativity that remains beyond all the grounding that it

37. Ibid, *GA* 65: 382 (§242).
38. Ibid., *GA* 65: 306 (§242).

enables, an originary concealment belonging to beyng and the event and decisively withheld beyond all grounding, the originary λήθη at the heart of ἀλήθεια.

Heidegger's engagement with the question of time-space and of its negativity does not cease after the account developed in *Contributions to Philosophy*. To take up the most decisive rethinking that Heidegger ventures in this regard, it is necessary to leap far beyond the series of texts discussed thus far.

Two and a half decades after he composed *Contributions to Philosophy*, Heidegger delivered the lecture "Time and Being." The title was provocative, as it was to have been the title of the never-published third Division of *Being and Time* in which the task of this work, to exhibit time as the meaning of being, would finally have been carried out. Yet, in a note to the published text of the lecture, Heidegger confesses that the lecture cannot be linked up with *Being and Time*, because in the intervening years the question, though still the same, has become still more questionable.

If "Time and Being" is compared with *Contributions to Philosophy*, what is most striking is that, in the lecture, grounding, which is so prominent in *Contributions to Philosophy*, plays no role whatsoever. As a result, the distinction that previously was drawn in various connections between ground and grounded is effaced, and the entire analysis now occurs on a plane where the separation between ground and grounded no longer occurs as such.

What is it, then, that replaces grounding or at least that compensates for this exclusion? It is what Heidegger calls *Reichen*—let us say *reaching* or *reaching out to*, though the word also has the sense of *holding out to, offering, extending to*. Yet, what figures in the lecture is not reaching in general but a single, unique, yet complex reaching. It is a reaching in which each of three moments reaches out to the others. The moments that are submitted to such reaching are those of time: future, past, and present.

What, then, is time-space? Heidegger defines it thus: "Time-space now names the open, which is cleared in the reaching in which future, past, and present reach out to one another."[39] Two points need to be noted in this definition. The first is that time-space is identified with the

---

39. Heidegger, *Zur Sache Des Denkens*, GA 14: 18f.

open, with the clearing. Here it is evident how grounding and the separation it entails have been eliminated: Whereas previously time-space was thought as the ground that grounds the open or clearing, now they are situated on the same level. Time-space *is* precisely the open that is cleared by way of the reaching. Yet, Heidegger identifies time-space not only with the open that is cleared but also—and this is the second point—with the complex of reachings by which the clearing is effected. In his words: "What is proper to the time-space of time proper lies in the reaching that clears, the reaching in which future, past, and present reach out to one another."[40] Thus, all—that is, time-space, the open or clearing, and the threefold reaching—not only operate on the same level but are so closely allied that each blends into the others.

Within this new configuration, the complex of reachings corresponds to the temporalization that, in *Contributions to Philosophy*, is effected by the abyssal grounding and, specifically, by the transport structure of time-space as the ground. But now, in "Time and Being," the temporalization merges with time-space rather than being—in any sense—grounded by it. It is as though the language of grounding has been replaced by one of sameness, of a sameness that does not simply—nor in the manner of an *Aufhebung*—exclude difference. To this extent the analysis of time-space has become an exercise in tautological thinking.

Though it is in "Time and Being" that Heidegger dismisses his attempt in *Being and Time* to trace Dasein's spatiality back to temporality, the lecture seems, in what little is said of space, to mark another dependence within the configuration developed in the lecture. Heidegger says that the reachings are pre-spatial and that it is only in this connection that there is space.

Much more developed than the question of space is that of the unity of the three reachings. Minimally expressed, their unity lies in the interplay (*Zuspiel*) of each with each. Heidegger regards this interplay itself as a fourth dimension along with the three that interplay; indeed, he regards the interplay itself to be the first of the four dimensions of time, since it is what draws future, past, and present near to one another by distancing them from one another.

Near the end of the lecture, Heidegger addresses, in effect, the question of negativity. Central to his account is the observation that in

---

40. Ibid., *GA* 14: 19.

the reaching to the past or the future, there is a refusal of the present, a withholding of the present. There is a hint of this refusal in the description of the past as no longer present and of the future as not yet present. The negativity that the word *not* here expresses Heidegger terms *Entzug*, withdrawal.

Toward the end of the lecture Heidegger brings the entire configuration that has taken shape—indeed far beyond these brief remarks—back to what he terms the oldest of the old in Western thought, namely, that which is held concealed in the word—which he hyphenates—ἀ-λήθεια. Here he evokes once more the originary *not*, the *not* that withdraws even from the word *Entzug* and that antecedes all grounding, that—so it seems—is anterior even to the *Ur-grund*, which in its designation retains reference to ground.

Near the end of one of his last published texts, "The End of Philosophy and the Task of Thinking," Heidegger asks how it is that ἀλήθεια has gone unthought. Is it—he asks rhetorically—something that has happened by chance or as a result of careless thinking? "Or does it happen because self-concealing, concealment, Λήθη, belongs to Ἀ-Λήθεια, not as a mere addition, not as shadow to light, but rather as the heart of Ἀλήθεια?"[41]

Finally, as a brief epilogue, let me propose a question, one that comes from outside Heidegger's analysis of time-space as abyssal ground or as a complex of reachings.

Throughout his analyses of time-space, Heidegger takes—in contrast to much of ancient thought—an uncompromising stand against mathematics or what he usually calls calculation. In one passage in *Contributions to Philosophy*, he declares that in calculation in its most powerful form, there is at work "the most indifferent and blindest denial of the incalculable."[42] It is as if a mathematical approach could never reach a point at which calculation might prove no longer possible. And yet, it is by no means evident that such an advance to incalculability is lacking in modern physics, for instance, in the discovery of such nonphenomenal phenomena as black holes and in Heisenberg's indeterminacy principle.[43]

---

41. Ibid., *GA* 14: 88.
42. Heidegger, *Beiträge zur Philosophie*, GA 65: 446 (§261)
43. See my discussion in "The Cosmological Turn," chap. 6 of *The Return of Nature: On the Beyond of Sense* (Bloomington: Indiana University Press, 2016).

THE NEGATIVITY OF TIME-SPACE   171

Near the end of the analysis of time-space in *Contributions to Philosophy*, Heidegger poses the question: "What is it about space and time that *allows* their mathematization?"[44] He immediately offers an answer: the condition that has made such mathematization possible is that the abyssal ground has been covered over—indeed, already in the first beginning.[45] And yet, the question is: In what Heidegger regards as the first beginning,[46] specifically with Plato, are there not ἀρχαί that are abyssal—most notably, τὸ ἀγαθόν as ἐπέκεινα τῆς οὐσίας and, indeed, most insistently, the χώρα?[47]

The χώρα is announced at the center of the *Timaeus*—if there be a center and to the extent that an announcement is possible. The dialogue is engaged with mathematics from the beginning, from the commencement of the counting—1, 2, 3,...—with which it begins. Both arithmetic and geometry serve to structure much of the description carried out in the first of Timaeus' three discourses. For example, in Timaeus' account of how the god formed the cosmic soul, shaping it into a long, harmoniously articulated band (which would prove to be the orbits of the heavenly bodies), he begins by declaring that as the first step the god took portions of the soul mixture corresponding to squares and cubes in the odd and even series of numbers.[48] Such theoretical reliance on mathematics runs throughout the first discourse, only to give way, when another beginning becomes imperative, to the chorology. In this discourse the χώρα proves to be incalculable and inaccessible (except through

---

44. Heidegger, *Beiträge zur Philosophie*, GA 65: 387 (§242).

45. Ibid., GA 65: 387 (§242).

46. The determination according to which there would have been a *first beginning* with which—through Plato—metaphysics would have commenced is put thoroughly into question, if not indeed undermined, by Heidegger's retraction of his Plato interpretation. Granting that ἀλήθεια was initially experienced only as ὀρθότης, Heidegger concludes: "But then the assertion about an essential transformation of truth, that is, from unconcealment to correctness, is also untenable" (*Zur Sache des* Denkens, GA 14: 87). Since it is precisely this alleged transformation that would constitute the first beginning, the very setting of *Contributions to Philosophy* between the first beginning and an other beginning cannot but be thoroughly displaced.

47. See my discussion with Jacques Derrida regarding the χώρα in its relation to what is ἐπέκεινα τῆς οὐσίας. The principal texts are (1) Jacques Derrida, "Tense," trans. D. F. Krell, in *The Path of Archaic Thinking: Unfolding the Work of John Sallis*, ed. Kenneth Maly (Albany: State University of New York Press, 1995); and (2) my text "Daydream," chap. 3 of *Platonic Legacies* (Albany: State University of New York Press, 2004).

48. Plato, *Timaeus*, 36a.

172   ELEMENTAL DISCOURSES

remembrance of a dream)—indeed to such an extent that the discourse itself is threatened with utter incoherence, with dissolution. Rather than preventing the advance toward the incalculable, the mathematics of the *Timaeus* leads the discourse precisely to the point where it breaks down and opens the space of what is abyssally incalculable.

In still another passage in *Contributions to Philosophy*, Heidegger explicitly contrasts time-space with the space and time of physics. Here again it is so-called calculation—that is, mathematical procedures—that is Heidegger's primary target. Such procedure—as he describes it—involves leveling space and time down to what is calculable and merely coupling them, merely tying them together. And yet, can one maintain that the special theory of relativity—along with its experimental confirmations—merely couples space and time, merely ties them together? For what this theory demonstrates is that the linear spatial movement of one thing with respect to another effects a difference in their time-determinations with regard to any particular event. Spatial movement, space as the medium of movement, is not merely tied together with temporal determination but is intrinsic to it. And this is to say nothing about the manner in which spatial distance between an earthbound observer and a distant galaxy brings about an enormous time-difference: in the present the observer sees the galaxy as it was in the very remote past.

The question is whether the results that modern physics has established regarding space and time have a bearing on the thinking of time-space; or whether these results are entirely undermined and rendered irrelevant for thinking by the role that mathematics plays in their formulation. Can the divide that Heidegger poses, the divide separating originary thinking from mathematical physics—separating it even from philosophy as determined in its Greek beginning—can this divide be crossed? Can the separation be overcome so that what modern physics has shown regarding space and time, along with what can be retrieved from ancient thought in its engagement with mathematics, can be brought to bear productively on the thinking of time-space? Might it be possible that through such a crossing the thinking that Heidegger has launched with such force might be brought to address, more affirmatively and more productively, that which most insistently confronts us in our time?

AFTERWORD

The papers on which the chapters of this volume of the *Collected Writings* (II/4) draw span the period from 1979 to 2017. Most of the more recent papers, previously unpublished, have been taken over more or less directly into the corresponding chapter. The earlier papers have been thoroughly reworked both in style and in content; since the corresponding chapters are only remotely related to the original papers, the titles have also been altered. The following list gives the provenance of each paper.

1. "Voices"—Presented at the Collegium Phaenomenologicum, 2015. Previously unpublished.
2. "Gathering Language"—Presented at Tongji University (Shanghai), 2015; and at Tunghai University (Taichung, Taiwan), 2015. Previously unpublished.
3. "The Play of Translation"—Draws on a paper presented as "Das Ende der Übersetzung" at the Heidegger Gesellschaft conference in Messkirch (Germany), 2003; presented as "The End of Translation" in Rio de Janeiro (Brazil), 2004; in Porto Alegre (Brazil), 2004; and at Memorial University of Newfoundland, 2004. German version of the original paper is published in *Dimensionen des Hermeneutischen* (Frankfurt a.M.: Vittorio Klostermann, 2005). English version is published in *Translation and the Classic*, ed. A. Lianeri and V. D. Zajko (Oxford University Press, 2007).
4. "Things of Sense"—Based on notes for a lecture presented as "The Thing and the Natural World" at the Collegium Phaenomenologicum, 1979.

5. "Archaic Nature"—Presented at the meeting of the Comparative and Continental Philosophy Circle, Phoenix, 2017. Previously unpublished.
6. "Alterity and the Elemental"—Draws on a paper published as "Levinas and the Elemental," *Research in Phenomenology*, 1998; reprinted in *Radicalizing Levinas*, ed. M. Calarco and P. Atterton (Albany: State University of New York Press, 2009).
7. "Objectivity and the Reach of Enchorial Space"—Draws on a paper presented as "On the Bounds and Expanse of Enchorial Space," Freiburg Institute for Advanced Studies, 2015. The paper was published as "Hermeneutics of Enchorial Space," *Epoché*, 2016; and as "Über Grenzen und Weite des enchorialen Raums," in *Raum Erfahren*, ed. D. Espinet, T. Keiling, N. Mirkovic (Tübingen: Mohr Siebeck, 2016).
8. "The Scope of Visibility"—Published as "The Extent of Visibility" in *Phenomenology and the Metaphysics of Sight*, ed. A. Cimino and P. Kontos (Leiden: Brill, 2014). I am grateful to Brill for permission to republish this paper.
9. "Cosmic Time"—Presented at the Collegium Phaenomenologicum, 2016. Previously unpublished.
10. "The Negativity of Time-Space"—Presented at meeting of the Heidegger Circle, Chicago, 2016. Previously unpublished.

I am grateful to my editor and friend Dee Mortensen for her encouragement and support. Thanks also to Nancy Fedrow, Christine Rojcewicz, and Stephen Mendelsohn for their very able and generous assistance.

John Sallis
Boston
October 2017

INDEX OF PRINCIPAL NAMES

Aristotle, 3–4, 7, 10–11, 13, 43, 47, 67, 161

Beethoven, Ludwig van, 123
Bernard, Émile, 14
Beston, Henry, 80
Bouquet, Carole, 18

Cicero, 41
Copernicus, 148

Derrida, Jacques, 4–16, 18, 152

Einstein, Albert, 150
Emerson, Ralph Waldo, 76–80, 83, 114–117

Feuerbach, Ludwig, 68–69
Fichte, Johann Gottlieb, 69–73, 76–77, 108–109, 114
Figal, Günter, 101, 106, 108, 110–111

Gadamer, Hans-Georg, 21, 46
Galileo, 123–124, 139, 147–148

Hegel, Georg Wilhelm Friedrich, 4, 47–50, 53, 71, 76, 102–103, 157–161, 164
Heidegger, Martin, 14–16, 21–35, 85–89, 91, 93, 103–111, 144–147, 151–172
Heraclitus, 61
Homer, 43–45, 141
Hubble, Edwin, 139, 148, 151,
Husserl, Edmund, 6, 7, 8–13, 61, 106, 112, 152

Jacobi, Friedrich Heinrich, 72, 77n23
Jacobson, Roman, 39

Kant, Immanuel, 1, 35, 58, 61, 68, 102–103, 111, 151
Klee, Paul, 82–83, 113
Kuki, Count Shuzo, 22–23, 26

Levinas, Emmanuel, 84–97

Marx, Karl, 68–69
Merleau-Ponty, Maurice, 52–64

Newton, Isaac, 148–151
Nietzsche, Friedrich, 100, 162

Plato, 21, 34, 43, 47, 171
Pope, Alexander, 43–46
Proclus, 42–43

Reinhold, Karl Leonhard, 101, 105

Schapiro, Meyer, 15
Schelling, Friedrich Wilhelm Joseph, 68–71, 72–76, 80, 83, 108
Socrates, 19, 34, 119, 126–136
Solon, 4, 40–41

Taylor, Thomas, 42–43
Thoreau, Henry David, 79–80
Timaeus, 42, 115–121, 124–125, 140, 143–144, 146–147, 152, 171–172

van Gogh, Vincent, 15

JOHN SALLIS is Frederick J. Adelmann Professor of Philosophy at Boston College. He is author of more than 20 books, including *Light Traces*, *The Return of Nature*, and *The Figure of Nature*.

www.ingramcontent.com/pod-product-compliance
Lightning Source LLC
Chambersburg PA
CBHW030655230426
43665CB00011B/1105